WORDSWORTH AND COLERIDGE

THE LYRICAL BALLADS

by

STEPHEN PRICKETT

Lecturer in English, School of English and American Studies,
University of Sussex

STIRLING
DISTRICT
LIBRARY

KU-308-892

EDWARD ARNOLD

© Stephen Prickett, 1975

B
2

First published 1975
by Edward Arnold (Publishers) Ltd,
25 Hill Street, London W1X 8LL

Cloth edition ISBN: 0 7131 5805 0
Paper edition ISBN: 0 7131 5806 9

All Rights Reserved. No part of this publication may be reproduced, stored in a retrieval system, or transmitted, in any form or by any means, electronic, mechanical, photocopying, recording or otherwise, without the prior permission of Edward Arnold (Publishers) Ltd.

This book is published in two editions. The paperback edition is sold subject to the condition that it shall not by way of trade or otherwise, be lent, resold, hired out, or otherwise circulated without the publisher's prior consent in any form of binding or cover other than that in which it is published and without a similar condition including this condition being imposed on the subsequent purchaser.

821.7
PRI

Printed in Great Britain by
The Camelot Press Ltd, Southampton

General Preface

The object of this series is to provide studies of individual novels, plays and groups of poems and essays which are known to be widely read by students. The emphasis is on clarification and evaluation; biographical and historical facts, while they may be discussed when they throw light on particular elements in a writer's work, are generally subordinated to critical discussion. What kind of work is this? What exactly goes on here? How good is this work, and why? These are the questions that each writer will try to answer.

It should be emphasized that these studies are written on the assumption that the reader has already read carefully the work discussed. The objective is not to enable students to deliver opinions about works they have not read, nor is it to provide ready-made ideas to be applied to works that have been read. In one sense all critical interpretation can be regarded as foisting opinions on readers, but to accept this is to deny the advantages of any sort of critical discussion directed at students or indeed at anybody else. The aim of these studies is to provide what Coleridge called in another context 'aids to reflection' about the works discussed. The interpretations are offered as suggestive rather than as definitive, in the hope of stimulating the reader into developing further his own insights. This is after all the function of all critical discourse among sensible people.

DAVID DAICHES

Contents

Author's Preface

Though the importance of the *Lyrical Ballads* as an event in our cultural history is widely acknowledged, the poems themselves have rarely been approached as an organic whole. Because we know that the original selection was in many cases arbitrary the possibility of there being an overall unity is usually ignored, in spite of evidence that Wordsworth and Coleridge saw the collection as a single aesthetic work. Similarly, 'The Ancient Mariner' is hardly ever seen in its context as the opening poem of the 1798 *Ballads*. In this brief book I have attempted to approach the *Lyrical Ballads* as an aesthetic unity that is particular and peculiar to the conditions under which it was produced in 1798—with Dorothy Wordsworth as a catalyst. My interpretation of the poems is very closely linked to the textual history and to the position of the poems in that first edition. The meaning of 'The Ancient Mariner' is seen as part of a unity that includes 'Tintern Abbey'. That is not to say I believe the poems to be the product of a carefully worked-out harmony of purpose, but rather that there was between Wordsworth and Coleridge a tension that, though essentially short-lived and unstable, was uniquely creative for both. Changes in their relationship, for instance, make the 1800 edition fundamentally different from the 1798 one. As I attempt to show in my final chapter, we can perhaps best understand the nature of this creative tension by looking at its fullest theoretical expression: the debate on poetic theory contained in Wordsworth's Prefaces of 1800 and 1802, and Coleridge's comments on them in the later chapters of *Biographia Literaria*. If I have been successful the whole study may throw some further light on Romantic theories of organic unity, 'reconciling opposite or discordant qualities'.

1   12 November 1797

By the time a collection of poems has acquired the status of being fit subject for critical studies in English literature, it is difficult for the reader to recapture any feelings of strangeness or novelty about its existence. Yet for contemporaries the *Lyrical Ballads* were both novel and very strange. If they had known the story behind this odd assortment of poems when it first appeared in 1798 they would have seen more clearly what a casual and ramshackle project its two authors had embarked upon. If we are to see the *Lyrical Ballads* in any sort of perspective, we must begin with their sheer oddity.

On 12 November 1797 Samuel Taylor Coleridge set out with William Wordsworth and his sister Dorothy to go on a walking-tour to the Valley of the Stones, a beauty-spot near Lynmouth in Devon. The two young poets were then near neighbours. Coleridge and his wife were renting a cottage in the Quantock village of Nether Stowey; the Wordsworths were living at Alfoxden, just outside the next village of Holford. All of them were desperately short of money. To choose to begin a walking-tour with insufficient money in the dark and seeping damp of an English November is eccentric enough, but to crown the absurdity of the whole enterprise, they did not set out until four in the afternoon—by daylight that must already have been fast fading. Their destination was the seaside town of Watchet. As a boy, Wordsworth had been accustomed to roaming the Furness fells in the Lake District all through the night; certainly walking the Quantocks by night is not to be recommended for beginners. 'The evening', says Dorothy Wordsworth, 'was dark and cloudy: we went eight miles, William and Coleridge employing themselves in laying the plan of a ballad, to be published with some pieces of William's.' Wordsworth's account gives a semblance of practicality by stressing the financial angle. 'As our united funds were very small, we agreed to defray the expense of the tour by writing a Poem, to be sent to the new Monthly Magazine set up by Phillips the bookseller and edited by Dr. Aikin.'[1]

'Magazine poetry' was then a recognized popular genre; the idea of paying for an excursion by an occasional and instantly profitable poem is

[1] Mary Moorman, *William Wordsworth*, I, 347.
Note: Titles listed in full in the bibliography are given in abbreviated form in footnotes.

every aspiring poet's fantasy—but from such an improbable beginning sprang 'The Ancient Mariner', and around it grew the whole edifice of the *Lyrical Ballads*. In the end it was to go through two editions and four printings, and to make for its authors a profit that by today's values would be undreamed of. Published in the first place anonymously by a small provincial bookseller, it was to make the poetic reputation (in varying degrees) of both poets, and it was to alter decisively the development of English poetry.

One can argue, of course, that this happenchance beginning was only the apparent excuse: that the real genesis of the *Lyrical Ballads* lay in the long-term poetic development of Wordsworth and Coleridge. The hastily-planned walking-tour to Lynmouth, so the argument might run, merely triggered off the poetic explosion which, backed as it was by a new aesthetic and poetic theory, lay like a time-bomb in the late 1790s. It was bound to have gone off sometime. Now there is obviously some truth in this kind of literary determinism, but the reason why I am choosing to stress the seemingly fortuitous and accidental quality of the development of the *Lyrical Ballads* is that real literary history—the moment one ceases to generalize in terms of aesthetic theory and poetic 'movements'—*is* much more complicated and accidental than even common sense would suggest. It is true that both Wordsworth and Coleridge at their best were, like nearly all great poets, also influential critics and aestheticians, but the creation of poetry is not in all respects like the overflowing spring of water with which they were so fond of comparing it. The 'spontaneous overflow of powerful feelings' is not subject to predictable laws of poetic hydrodynamics. In other words, there is not so much poetry present like water in the ground of a poet's mind that will somehow force its way to the surface and which, if one exit is blocked, will find its way through another. For Wordsworth, of course, the word 'spontaneous' still carried its older meaning from the Latin root *sua sponte*: 'of one's own accord' or 'willingly'. The poetic feelings he is describing are generated by the poet's own desire—they are neither involuntary and automatic (as the modern word can suggest) nor the product of external stimulus. For Wordsworth, the 'powerful feelings' of the poet are the creation of his unified *purpose*. Thus poetry is particular. It is actual, not latent. The occasion of a poem, for the Romantics, was part of the poem itself. 'Tintern Abbey' was important to Wordsworth because he *had* been there five years before in very different circumstances, and the same assurances of Nature's healing power given as a generalized truth would have resulted in a very different (and probably less good) poem. For the writing of the *Lyrical Ballads* it is important that Wordsworth and Coleridge were together at this particular moment in history.

Both poets wrote verse when they were not in close contact with each other—before 1797, and after their tragic quarrel in 1810—but the poetry of each that we remember comes from those few years when, with Dorothy, 'three hearts beat as one'. Wordsworth and Coleridge needed each other, even when they argued, in order that they might be fully themselves. Coleridge, without Wordsworth, was not fully Coleridge. Now, in the Quantocks in 1797, he was just beginning his 'annus mirabilis'—the year in which nearly all his finest poems were written. 'Kubla Khan', 'The Ancient Mariner', 'This Lime-tree Bower my Prison', 'Frost at Midnight', and the first part of 'Christabel' all date from this period of close friendship with William and Dorothy in 1797–8. Only 'Dejection' comes from a later period, 1802, when, although the friends were seemingly as close as ever, already Coleridge's ruinous marriage was beginning to obtrude. The title speaks for itself. Coleridge's trip to Malta from 1804–6, undertaken for the sake of his health and to escape from his wife, was a disaster in personal terms, and by 1810 he had more or less ceased to write poetry of any significance. It is interesting that his last important poem was written at his reunion with Wordsworth at Coleorton in January 1807, and was inspired by hearing recited the poem 'on the growth of an individual mind'—later to be called *The Prelude*. It was a work to which Coleridge himself had contributed much, and his reaction sums up their relationship: 'as I listened with a heart forlorn, / The pulses of my being beat anew:' (ll. 61–2).

Without the renewal of Coleridge's presence and his constant flow of letters, Wordsworth continued to write poetry, indeed his craftsmanship is often of a high order, but few who compare the poems written for or in the company of Coleridge with those of his later years can doubt the crucial effect of this friendship on his work. Wordsworth, for all his painstakingness, was a poet of genius rather than talent. When he is not sublime, he is frequently trivial, sententious, and dull. Indeed, his peculiar genius—often seen at its best in the poems of the *Lyrical Ballads*—lies in living dangerously. The strength of 'We are seven' or 'An Anecdote for Fathers' is that the possibility of the banal is always present, and, in these poems, it is always magnificently avoided. Some have claimed the same successful tension for 'Simon Lee', but in my opinion this poem shows us rather how close Wordsworth constantly is to absurdity by crossing the line. It is for me, an awful reminder of how precarious is his tightrope act elsewhere.

To maintain this fragile poise that is so typical of Wordsworth at his best, he needed not merely Coleridge but Dorothy. She was the third essential ingredient in the walking-tour that began in the dusk of that November evening of 1797. In Book X of *The Prelude* (1805 version) Wordsworth describes in most moving terms the parts played by Coleridge (the 'most precious friend') and Dorothy in his recovery and regeneration from despair after the collapse of all his hopes in the French Revolution:

>   Ah! then it was
> That thou, most precious Friend! about this time
> First known to me, didst lend a living help
> To regulate my Soul, and then it was
> That the beloved Woman in whose sight
> Those days were passed, now speaking in a voice
> Of sudden admonition—like a brook
> That does but *cross* a lonely road, and now
> Seen, heard and felt, and caught at every turn,
> Companion never lost through many a league—
> Maintained for me a saving intercourse
> With my true self; for, though impaired and changed
> Much, as it seemed, I was no further changed
> Than as a clouded, not a waning moon:
> She, in the midst of all, preserved me still
> A Poet, made me seek beneath that name
> My office upon earth, and nowhere else;
> And, lastly, Nature's self, by human love
> Assisted, through the weary labyrinth
> Conducted me again to open day,
> Revived the feelings of my early life. . . .   (ll. 905–25)

Wordsworth has, perhaps, too easily been credited with being *par excellence* the 'poet of Nature'. We are apt to forget that (as he reminds us in *The Prelude*) he came to his love of Nature through his love of man—and that it was Coleridge and, even more, Dorothy who enabled him to make the connection. Wordsworth's vision of Nature remained to a very curious degree a generalized and symbolic one, even when he is writing about a specific place or object, as if he was always more interested in looking for a meaning *in* Nature than in seeing it for its individuality and uniqueness. Thus we find the odd paradox that Coleridge's description of the water-snakes in the Pacific (which he knew only at second-hand through his reading and whose purpose is overtly symbolic) is more vivid and memorable than Wordsworth's descriptions of marvels that he had seen and whose purpose is to re-create the scene with visionary intensity. A comparison between the 'Ancient Mariner' and the 'Immortality Ode' highlights this difference. Equally, in the realm of familiar, everyday objects—supposedly Wordsworth's forte—Coleridge or Dorothy can re-create their memories with greater intensity. Coleridge's 'conversation poem', 'The Nightingale', which was included in the first edition of the *Lyrical Ballads* at the last minute, is a slight poem, but it contains passages of acutely observed natural description that Wordsworth never equalled in far better poems. There is nothing in 'Tintern Abbey', for instance, to compare in descriptive detail with:

> This grove is wild with tangling underwood,
> And the trim walks are broken up, and grass,
> Thin grass and king-cups grow within the paths.
> But never elsewhere in one place I knew
> So many Nightingales . . .
>
>   . . . On moonlight bushes,
> Whose dewy leafits are but half disclos'd,
> You may perchance behold them on the twigs,
> Their bright, bright eyes, their eyes both bright and full,
> Glistening, while many a glow-worm in the shade
> Lights up her love torch.   (ll. 51-5; 64-9)

Coleridge's eye is attuned to pick out particularity; he fastens on the unusual and exceptional. Wordsworth is being no less precise in observing the scenery of the Wye valley above Tintern. He notes the point where the river ceases to be tidal, for instance. But his vision is not exceptional, but normative:

>   Once again I see
> These hedge-rows, hardly hedge-rows, little lines
> Of sportive wood run wild; these pastoral farms
> Green to the very door;   (ll. 15–18)

This is not a landscape observed simply for its own sake: it is the carefully controlled backdrop for what follows, which is a poem of ideas. Perhaps even more striking, since it involves a comparison of like with like, is the contrast between Dorothy's descriptions and those of her brother. Wordsworth's poem 'The Daffodils' is a masterpiece of its kind, and one of the most succinct philosophical statements on 'Nature' that he ever made—only comparable, perhaps, with 'The Tables Turned'. I quote from the last and fullest version of the poem:

> I wandered lonely as a cloud
> That floats on high o'er vales and hills,
> When all at once I saw a crowd,
> A host, of golden daffodils;
> Beside the lake, beneath the trees,
> Fluttering and dancing in the breeze.
>
> Continuous as the stars that shine
> And twinkle on the milky way,
> They stretched in never-ending line
> Along the margin of the bay:
> Ten thousand saw I at a glance,
> Tossing their heads in sprightly dance.

But we only have to compare this with his sister's entry in her journal for 15 April 1802 to see not merely how Wordsworth has transposed the original experience in order to create from it a poem (claiming, for instance, to be alone), but also simply how much *better* an observer and recorder Dorothy could be:

> When we were in the woods beyond Gowbarrow Park we saw a few daffodils close to the water-side. We fancied that the lake had floated the seeds ashore, and that the little colony had so sprung up. But as we went along there were more and yet more; and at last, under the boughs of the trees, we saw that there was a long belt of them along the shore, about the breadth of a country turnpike road. I never saw daffodils so beautiful. They grew among the mossy stones about and about them; some rested their heads upon these stones as on a pillow for weariness; and the rest tossed and reeled and danced, and seemed as if they verily laughed with the wind, that blew upon them over the lake; they looked so gay, ever glancing, ever changing. This wind blew directly over the lake to them. There was here and there a little knot, and a few stragglers a few yards higher up; but they were so few as not to disturb the simplicity, unity, and life of that one busy highway.

Dorothy was not a poet. She was writing in her private journal for the interest only of family and close friends (such as Coleridge), but this unpolished account has an immediacy and vitality that her brother, drawing on this account five years later, could not match.

When in the *Lyrical Ballads* we do find Wordsworth attempting detailed natural descriptions of particular objects, it is, in contrast with his two companions, strongly anthropomorphic. In 'The Thorn', for instance, in order to describe the tree to us at all he has to humanize it, making it as much like a person as possible:

> There is a thorn; it looks so old,
> In truth you'd find it hard to say,
> How it could ever have been young,
> It looks so old and grey.
> Not higher than a two-years' child,
> It stands erect this aged thorn;
> No leaves it has, no thorny points;
> It is a mass of knotted joints,
> A wretched thing forlorn.
> It stands erect, and like a stone
> With lichens it is overgrown.
>
> Like rock or stone, it is o'ergrown
> With lichens to the very top,
> And hung with heavy tufts of moss,
> A melancholy crop:
> Up from the earth these mosses creep,
> And this poor thorn they clasp it round
> So close, you'd say that they were bent
> With plain and manifest intent,
> To drag it to the ground;
> And all had joined in one endeavour
> To bury this poor thorn for ever.   (ll. 1–22)

The truth is, at this stage in his life Wordsworth had no great interest in Nature for its own sake, but only in its metaphorical role as a way of talking about the complexities of man. The 'otherness' and strangeness of Nature so cherished in the poetry of Coleridge or Gerard Manley Hopkins, which prevented them from ever degenerating into the kind of feeble pathetic fallacy we find in 'The Thorn', seems to have passed him by. It is doubtful, indeed, if Wordsworth ever acquired the quality of feeling for Nature possessed by Coleridge or Dorothy. His finest descriptions of natural scenery (in 'Tintern Abbey', for instance, or the beginning of Book XIII of the 1805 *Prelude*) occur where the landscape seems to chime in with the poet's own mood, and so offers him a way of talking about himself. In the 1800 edition of the *Lyrical Ballads* a second

volume of poems was added which included this very revealing account
of himself in a poem called 'Nutting'.

> A little while I stood,
> Breathing with such suppression of the heart
> As joy delights in; and with wise restraint
> Voluptuous, fearless of a rival, eyed
> The banquet . . .
>
>   Then up I rose,
> And dragg'd to earth both branch and bough, with crash
> And merciless ravage; and the shady nook
> Of hazels, and the green and mossy bower
> Deform'd and sullied, patiently gave up
> Their quiet being: and unless I now
> Confound my present feelings with the past,
> Even then, when from the bower I turn'd away,
> Exulting, rich beyond the wealth of kings
> I felt a sense of pain when I beheld
> The silent trees and the intruding sky.—   (ll. 20–4; 42–52)

The language of 'rape' used for the destruction of that woodland bower
by an act of wanton vandalism is followed at once by an instinctive 'pain'
and shame that tells us how far his real motives were from simply
gathering nuts. Such glimpses into the human desire for violence and
destruction tell us more about the nature of man than either the rational
empirical psychology of the day, or Wordsworth's own efforts at rustic
psychology in 'Goody Blake and Harry Gill' or 'Simon Lee'. It offers us a
darker meaning to those lines from 'The Tables Turned':

> One impulse from a vernal wood
> May teach you more of man;
> Of moral evil and of good,
> Than all the sages can.   (ll. 21–4)

The qualities of the *Lyrical Ballads*: an acute observation of Nature
coupled with a no less acute insight into the irrational complexities of
human behaviour, are not qualities about which we can easily generalize.
For one thing, as we have seen, the level of the poems varies wildly: the
material of genius is also, to a peculiar degree with Wordsworth, the
material of banality. Their qualities do not spring from a fully-developed
philosophic or aesthetic position common to the two poets—though they
would have been impossible without some such framework. Still less are
they common to the whole range of the two poets' collaboration. The

relationship of Wordsworth and Coleridge was something in a constant state of change and flux. Even by the time of the 1800 edition of the *Lyrical Ballads*, as we shall see, their relationship was very different from what it had been three years earlier. In *The Prelude*, 'Dejection', or the 'Immortality Ode' their interaction showed itself in ways that were very different again—even within the space of a few months. We can see very clearly the uniqueness and particularity of that November dusk of 1797 if we look at the story and subsequent history of 'The Ancient Mariner'—the germ and original centrepiece of the whole project.

To begin with, the basis of the 'plot', that is, the Mariner's crime, his guilt, and expiation, are not the invention of Coleridge at all, but of Wordsworth. He tells us that:

> Much the greatest part of the story was Mr. Coleridge's invention; but certain parts I myself suggested, for example, some crime was to be committed which should bring upon the Old Navigator, as Coleridge afterwards delighted to call him, the spectral persecution, as a consequence of that crime, and his own wanderings. I had been reading in Shelvock's *Voyages* a day or two before that while doubling Cape Horn they frequently saw Albatrosses in that latitude, the largest sort of sea-fowl, extending their wings 12 or 13 feet. 'Suppose', said I, 'you represent him as having killed one of these birds on entering the South Sea, and that the tutelary Spirits of these regions take upon them to avenge the crime.' The incident was thought fit for the purpose and adopted accordingly. I also suggested the navigation of the ship by the dead man, but I do not recollect that I had anything more to do with the scheme of the poem. . . . We began the composition on that, to me, memorable evening. I furnished two or three lines at the beginning of the poem, in particular:

> > And listened like a three years' child;
> > The Mariner hath his will.[2]

The theme was one in many ways closer to Wordsworth's heart than to Coleridge's. Ever since his return from France, disillusioned with the way the French Revolution had turned out, crime, guilt, and punishment had been an obsession with Wordsworth. This is the theme of *The Borderers*, a verse drama, and his only play, which he had begun the year before in 1796. Another attempt at a collaborative poem with Coleridge, 'The Three Graves', also reveals the same preoccupations. Like many of their joint projects, it was never completed.

Paradoxically, neither poet in fact found collaboration easy. Some of

[2] Moorman, I, 348.

the best lines in 'The Ancient Mariner' are by Wordsworth. In addition to the two lines cited above, Coleridge himself acknowledged Wordsworth's authorship of the lines at the end of the first stanza of Part IV: 'And thou art long and lank and brown / As is the ribbed sea sand.' The unwary reader might well be forgiven for picking these out as typically 'Coleridgean' lines. Yet this very apparent success in blending their two styles in 'The Ancient Mariner' also illustrates the precarious nature of even such enthusiastically-given co-operation. Later that evening, after their arrival at Watchet for the night, the two friends tried to go on with their poem. 'Our respective manners,' said Wordsworth afterwards, 'proved so widely different that it would have been quite presumptuous in me to do anything but separate from an undertaking upon which I could only have been a clog.' It was this ability of the two poets simultaneously both to collaborate and conflict that characterized not merely 'The Ancient Mariner' but the whole enterprise of the *Lyrical Ballads*. On other occasions it was to lead to increasing disharmony and frustration; here, the peculiar genius of the poem seems to be a direct creation of the tension which was to prove so disastrous elsewhere. In effect, 'The Ancient Mariner' has not one, but *two* authors. Neither could have produced it alone. Though they could produce common work elsewhere, it is of a quite different order. A number of poems Coleridge published under his name in the *Morning Post* are now known to be either direct transcripts or reworkings of earlier poems by Wordsworth. Perhaps the most striking example of Coleridge 'cannibalizing' material by Wordsworth is in his poem 'Lewti' which was originally intended for inclusion in the *Lyrical Ballads*, but, since it had already appeared signed by Coleridge in the *Morning Post*, was finally replaced at the last minute in most copies by 'The Nightingale'. 'Lewti' is, in fact, a reworking and enlargement of a poem by Wordsworth called 'Beauty and Moonshine'. Such re-use of Wordsworthian material by Coleridge is utterly different from what is going on in 'The Ancient Mariner', and illustrates very graphically by comparison the uniqueness of November 1797.

By the following spring the two poets turned again to plans for joint publication of a collection of poems to include 'The Ancient Mariner'. It must, they insisted to their publisher, Cottle, be produced jointly and anonymously. Coleridge wrote to explain that they regarded 'the volumes offered to you as to a certain degree one work, in kind, though not in degree, as an ode in one work; and that our different poems are as stanzas, good, relatively rather than absolutely.' Cottle disliked the idea of anonymity, but they insisted. One reason, argued Coleridge, was that 'Wordsworth's name is nothing, and mine stinks'—presumably from his political activities. The other reason is more interesting from our point of view. It was that both poets saw the *Lyrical Ballads* as a particular kind of artistic unity that would be lost on many readers if it were known that the poems were by two different authors. In *Biographia Literaria* Coleridge describes the plan as it gradually emerged from their discussions:

> The thought suggested itself (to which of us I do not recollect) that a series of poems might be composed of two sorts. In the one, the incidents and agents were to be, in part at least, supernatural; and the excellence aimed at was to consist in the interesting of the affections by the dramatic truth of such emotions, as would naturally accompany such situations, supposing them real. . . . For the second class, subjects were to be chosen from ordinary life; the characters and incidents were to be such as will be found in every village and its vicinity, where there is a meditative and feeling mind to seek after them, or notice them, when they present themselves.
>
> In this idea originated the plan of the *Lyrical Ballads*; in which it was agreed that my endeavours should be directed to persons and characters supernatural, or at least romantic; yet so as to transfer from our inward nature a human interest and a semblance of truth sufficient to procure for these shadows of imagination that willing suspension of disbelief for the moment, which constitutes poetic faith. Mr. Wordsworth, on the other hand, was to propose to himself as his object, to give the charm of novelty to things every day, and to excite a feeling analogous to the supernatural, by awakening the mind's attention from the lethargy of custom, and directing it to the loveliness and the wonders of the world before us; an inexhaustible treasure, but for which, in consequences of the film of familiarity and selfish solicitude we have eyes, yet not see, ears that hear not, and hearts that neither feel nor understand.[3]

However, Coleridge confesses, Wordsworth's 'industry proved so much more successful, and the number of his poems so much greater, that my compositions, instead of forming a balance, appeared rather an interpolation of heterogeneous matter'. This is something of an exaggeration, since in the first edition Coleridge's contributions amounted to one-third of the total number of pages. What is true is that by the spring of 1798 Coleridge's own need for money was much less pressing than it had been the previous autumn. The Wedgwood family, with the idea of encouraging genius, had given him an annuity of £150. Ironically his new affluence meant he had less need to publish. In addition

[3] *Biographia Literaria*, J. Shawcross, II, 5–6.

to the disproportionately long 'Ancient Mariner' and 'The Nightingale', the only other poems of his to appear in this first edition of the *Lyrical Ballads* were 'The Foster-Mother's Tale' and 'The Dungeon' both of which were lifted from his tragedy 'Osorio'.

Wordsworth kept his part of the bargain with a number of much shorter poems. While for the most part these do observe the aim of displaying the 'characters and incidents such as will be found in every village', they can hardly be described as 'ballads' in any more recognizable sense than Coleridge's contributions. It has been claimed that 'Goody Blake and Harry Gill', 'The Idiot Boy', and 'The Thorn' are, at least, 'real ballads'. But even this claim is to interpret 'ballad' in a fairly generous sense. Wordsworth and Coleridge were both familiar with Percy's *Reliques*, a collection of ballads and other old poems that had led to a tremendous revival of interest in the form during the late eighteenth century. The fourth edition of the *Reliques* had appeared in 1794. A number of much less original poets had imitated the genre with considerable success, and it is inconceivable that Wordsworth and Coleridge were not well enough aware of how different even 'The Ancient Mariner' was from the traditional models. In his Advertisement to the first edition of the *Lyrical Ballads* Wordsworth seems to be admitting this when he stresses that the poems are to be 'considered as experiments'. His comments seem to imply that they are intended as 'experiments' in diction and in theme, but it would be no less true to describe them as metrical experiments. If they are not ballads in Percy's antiquarian sense, neither were they lyrics in any sense familiar to contemporary readers. Others, like Cowper or Blake, had already broken with the rhymed couplet that was the norm of eighteenth-century verse, but in 1798 the sheer variety of metres and styles encompassed deliberately in the one slim volume seemed to readers wilfully eccentric. However one takes the word 'ballad', it does not include the use of blank verse. Wordsworth's choice of this verse form in 'Tintern Abbey', coupled with Coleridge's use of it in his conversation poems, heralds the second great age of blank verse in English.

Surprisingly, for us, the least original facet of the *Lyrical Ballads* is the range of subject-matter. The 'magazine poetry' of the period was full of poems on the beauties of Nature or the sufferings of the innocent. Bereaved and abandoned mothers, or hapless beggars were the standard stuff of an age which only a few years before had coined the new word 'sentimental' to describe its growing interest in the cultivation of the feelings. What Wordsworth did was to take the stock figures of an age of affectation and hyper-sensibility to recharge them with first-hand emotions. Through his own involvement in the French Revolution and his unhappy love affair with Annette Vallon he had come to a new and deeper sympathy with the failures and outcasts of a society that had institutionalized harshness and injustice towards its weakest members. There is nothing sentimental—even in its eighteenth-century sense—about Wordsworth's patriotic indignation at seeing a man in tears on a public road in 'The Last of the Flock'.

Perhaps it was as well that Wordsworth and Coleridge had both gone for a prolonged stay in Germany by the time the *Lyrical Ballads* were finally published in the autumn of 1798, for their poems were not well received by the critics. 'The Ancient Mariner', with which the volume opened, was an obvious target for reviewers looking in vain for familiar territory—and they did not pull their punches. It has 'more of the extravagance of a mad German poet than of the simplicity of our ancient ballad writers' declared the *Analytical Reivew*[4] (quite correctly). More mysterious was opinion of the *Monthly Review* that it was 'the strangest story of a cock and a bull that we ever saw on paper', but it then relented far enough to admit that it did contain 'poetical touches of an exquisite kind'.[5] Southey, also an aspiring poet who was Coleridge's brother-in-law and had been one of his closest friends, reviewed the *Ballads* anonymously in the *Critical Review*. 'The Ancient Mariner' was, he said, 'a Dutch attempt at German sublimity' and he found the story 'absurd and unintelligible'.[6] 'Tintern Abbey', however, he praised highly, merely lamenting that its author should have 'condescended to write such pieces as the "Last of the Flock", "The Convict", and most of the ballads'. 'The "experiment",' he concluded, not without relish, 'has failed . . . because it has been tried upon uninteresting subjects.' Almost the only periodical to praise the *Lyrical Ballads* was the *British Critic*, whose reviewer was Francis Wrangham, a fellow poet and a friend of both Wordsworth and Coleridge. He alone among the reviewers seems to have grasped what the *Lyrical Ballads* were attempting to do. 'It is not pomp of words, but by energy of thought,' he tells us, 'that sublimity is most successfully achieved.' For him 'the simplicity of even the most unadorned tale in this volume' is preferable to 'all the meretricious frippery' of current taste.[7]

Perhaps aided by this timely boost from Wrangham, the *Lyrical Ballads* did in fact sell better than had at first been feared, and by June 1800 the first edition had sold out. Cottle had retired, but Longman, the London publisher who had taken over all his copyrights in 1799, and who had

[4] *Lyrical Ballads*, 320.   [5] *Ibid.*, 321.
[6] *Ibid.*, 320.   [7] *Ibid.*, 324.

then thought the *Ballads* worthless, was now sufficiently impressed to offer £80 for the rights to the existing volume—for another 'of the same size' to be added. This, together with the 30 guineas each poet had been paid for the first edition, meant that the project had in the end made its authors a considerable amount of money. It is difficult to compare prices with the present day, but if we take it that Wedgwood's annuity of £150 was enough for a family to live on, then Longman's offer was at least half a year's salary. No poet today could expect to make that kind of money from a first volume.

As we have seen, the new edition was to be a much more ambitious two-volume affair. The planning of this, and the third edition of 1802, illustrate very clearly the ever-shifting relationship between Words-worth and Coleridge. Already it had altered in ways that were to mean there could be no repetition of that evening in November 1797. Perhaps with unintended symbolism, the fate of 'The Ancient Mariner' itself was in doubt. Wordsworth had never been quite happy about the finished result, and the attacks of critics (though they made no impression on his opinion of his own work) had given him further doubts about Coleridge's poem. 'From what I can gather it seems that The Ancyent Marinere has upon the whole been an injury to the volume,' he wrote in June 1799,[8] and at first he seemed determined to leave it out altogether. His own reputation was now much more clearly at stake—the new edition was to be published entirely under his name. There had been talk of 'Christabel' going into the new volume, but in the event Coleridge had contributed nothing to it. One poem, entitled 'Love', was substituted for Wordsworth's 'The Convict' in the first volume. In a spirit of almost masochistic self-abasement Coleridge had insisted that Wordsworth, not he, was 'the great, the true Poet' and nothing must be allowed to detract from his friend's glory. In the end, the text of 'The Ancient Mariner' was substantially revised (much to its advantage), and it was moved from its former prominence to a less conspicuous position at the end of the first volume. In addition, as if to wash his hands of it the more thoroughly, Wordsworth added a note to assure the reader that he was not its author. He went on to suggest solemnly that it might be helpful if the reader imagines the story to be told by the superstitious and talkative retired 'Captain of a small trading vessel'. It is hard to imagine, under the guise of co-operation, a more drastic transformation of the spirit of joint authorship that had inspired the poem only three years before.

Finally, Wordsworth added his famous Preface: a much more lengthy

[8] Letter to Cottle, 24 June 1799. *Letters of William and Dorothy Wordsworth: The Early Years*, ed. E. de Selincourt and C. L. Shaver, 264 (no. 117).

poetic manifesto than the brief and cautiously apologetic Advertisement that graced the first edition. It is a document of central importance in understanding the *Lyrical Ballads*, and it will be treated at length in the third chapter of this book. How far Wordsworth was stating his own views, and how far he is still speaking for Coleridge as well has always been a matter of conjecture. Coleridge was not averse to implying that many of its ideas were really his own in origin; on the other hand in *Biographia Literaria* he is sharply critical of some parts of the Preface—most notably Wordsworth's theory of poetic diction. During the period 1797–8 it is obvious that the two poets developed their ideas with such passionate interplay that in retrospect they had the greatest difficulty in saying who had first thought of what. It is equally clear, however, that the 1800 *Lyrical Ballads* is a different *kind* of book from its predecessor. It is still a collaborative effort, but the nature of that collaboration was no longer spontaneous, unforced, and open-ended: capable of developing into something individually beyond the reach of either. For better or worse, Wordsworth was in control now, and Coleridge was merely his assistant. The Preface proclaimed the new aesthetic theory—and poems such as 'The Ancient Mariner' which did not easily fit the declared pattern were explicitly disowned. Many of the poems in the second volume are good poems, but none of them is of the genius of 'Tintern Abbey' or 'The Ancient Mariner'. The *Lyrical Ballads* went on to further commercial success—it was reprinted in 1802 (with substantial additions to the Preface), and again in 1805—but the moment that had created it was past and irrecoverable.

2 Unity with Diversity

So much for the barebones story of the *Lyrical Ballads*. But what of the poems themselves? We have already seen how hard it was for contemporary readers and reviewers to grapple with the central paradox of this immodest collection of verses: that this diversity of themes and styles had a life and unity which depended on the very tensions of a tight-rope act in which the safety-net was first removed. If their point was to be made at all, 'The Idiot Boy', 'The Mad Mother', or 'Simon Lee' had to be about people or incidents that were trivial, trite, or grotesque. More-over, they had to be part of the same grand design that included 'The Ancyent Marinere' as its starting point, and 'Tintern Abbey' as its conclusion. It is my argument in this book that there *is* such a 'life' and 'grand design' to the *Lyrical Ballads* even while it can be shown that it was never fully present in either of its authors' heads at the same time—if at all. To show this unity with diversity it would not be possible (nor even desirable) to discuss every one of the shifting group of poems which appeared at some time in the various editions. What I intend to do, therefore, is to look in some detail at a relatively small number of what I consider to be the most important poems, in particular of the first edition, to see how they relate to the overall unity that Wordsworth and Coleridge themselves only half-glimpsed, and which nevertheless, by some miracle, gives life to the whole.

The Ancient Mariner

'The Ancient Mariner' has suffered from familiarity in two ways. The first is that it no longer has for us the shock of instant pecularity that it held for its first readers in 1798. The second is that we read it in isolation, and no longer encounter it as the starting-point (in both senses) of the *Lyrical Ballads*. We must begin by trying to perform the impossible task of seeing what those early critics and readers found when they opened their copies of the first edition and were confronted not by our familiar 'Ancient Mariner', but by the much more exotic 'Rime of the Ancyent Marinere'—a text boldly studded with the most extraordinary bogus spellings and archaisms. The marginal gloss which we now take for

granted was absent: that was not added until Coleridge's final version of
the poem in 1817. There were some extra verses. For instance, the spectre
bark has a crew of gothick horror far more graphic and grotesque than in
the later version. Death is a skeleton:

> *His* bones were black with many a crack,
> All black and bare, I ween;
> Jet black and bare, save where with rust
> Of mouldy damps and charnel crust
> They're patch'd with purple and green . . .   (ll. 181–5)

> A gust of wind sterte up behind
> And whistled thro' his bones;
> Thro' the holes of his eyes and the hole of his mouth,
> Half-whistles and half groans.   (ll. 195–8)

In the 1800 text all this superfluous bone-rattling was omitted. At the
same point some of the best-known and most beautiful stanzas were
added. This, for instance, near the beginning:

> With sloping masts and dipping prow,
> As who pursued with yell and blow
> Still treads the shadow of his foe,
> And forward bends his head,
> The ship drove fast, loud roared the blast,
> And southward aye we fled.   (ll. 45–50)

or this, in Part III:

> We listened and looked sideways up!
> Fear at my heart, as at a cup,
> My life-blood seemed to sip!
> The stars were dim, and thick the night,
> The steersman's face by his lamp gleamed white;
> From the sails the dew did drip—   (ll. 203–8)

We must bear these changes in mind when we read of the critics'
incomprehension and dislike of 'The Ancient Mariner', and remember
that they were confronted in 1798 with what was, in many superficial
ways, a startlingly different poem. Yet even had these puzzled critics from
the *Monthly*, *Critical*, or *Analytical Reviews* been faced with the revised and
improved text of 1800, instead of that of 1798, we should not
underestimate their difficulties. What, after all, *is* the poem all about? Is it
simply a tale of mystery and imagination, or is there a meaning and a

purpose to it that links it—however tenuously—to the didactic moralizing of so many of the other poems? 'The Ancient Mariner' certainly has a perfectly good moral in the proper place—at the end of the poem:

> O sweeter than the Marriage-feast
> 'Tis sweeter far to me,
> To walk together to the Kirk
> With a goodly company!—
>
> To walk together to the Kirk
> And all together pray,
> While each to his great Father bends,
> Old men, and babes, and loving friends
> And Youths and Maidens gay!
>
> Farewel, farewell! but this I tell
> To thee, thou Wedding·Guest!
> He prayeth well, who loveth well
> Both man and bird and beast.
>
> He prayeth best, who loveth best
> All things both great and small;
> For the dear God who loveth us,
> He made and loveth all.   (ll. 634–50)

These lines are reprinted with unaltered words in the 1800 edition. Unity with Nature and living things is also unity with God. There is a surprising similarity of tone between these sentiments and some of the simpler of Wordsworth's morals in the *Ballads*. At the most superficial level, therefore, it can be argued that 'The Ancient Mariner' fulfils Coleridge's part of the original design: the marvellous and supernatural takes its place beside the incidents of everyday life to uphold a single universal morality.

But how sure can we be that this *is* the 'moral' of the poem? As an old man in 1830 Coleridge made a very curious remark to Mrs Barbauld—a celebrated, and now forgotten, lady poetess. She had said to him that the poem had no moral. He replied that, on the contrary, it had too much of a moral!

> . . . and that the only, or chief fault, if I might say so, was the obtrusion of the moral sentiment so openly on the reader as a principle or cause of action in a work of such pure imagination. It ought to have had no more moral than the Arabian Nights tale of the merchant's

sitting down to eat dates by the side of a well, and throwing the shells aside, and lo! a genie starts up, and says he *must* kill the aforesaid merchant, *because* one of the date shells had, it seems, put out the eye of the genie's son.[1]

Poets' comments thirty years afterwards are not always to be trusted, but Coleridge's remark must at least be taken seriously. Certainly, *if* that passage at the end of 'The Ancient Mariner' is the moral, then it must be acknowledged that it is a very curious one. It seems to raise more moral problems than it satisfies. It is surely not self-evident from the story that God loves us all. For instance, what about the other sailors who, because they condone the Mariner's crime, are condemned to die horribly of thirst? If we follow the logic of the poem, then the only clear unequivocal message is that it is unwise to shoot albatrosses.

Some critics have indeed found the poem profoundly pessimistic. D. W. Harding, for example, sees the Mariner as a ruined man: 'Creeping back defeated into the social convoy, the mariner is obviously not represented as having advanced through his sufferings to a fuller life; and he no more achieves a full rebirth than Coleridge ever could.'[2] Clearly, in the light of the whole poem, that great religious affirmation of love and unity at the end is much more ambiguous than it would appear. Is the Mariner's final state really one of irreparable damage—as Harding argues? If so, then the ending must be not a statement of what he has *found*, but what he has *lost* for ever by his guilt. Alternatively, can we say that he achieves through his suffering such insight as leaves him 'no longer at ease here in the old dispensation'? Or again, is the Mariner now able to rejoin his fellows at the church just *because* of his new and terrible knowledge? In T. S. Eliot's words:

> the end of all our exploring,
> Will be to arrive where we started
> And know the place for the first time.

The ideal that is celebrated in those final stanzas—'to walk together to the kirk'—seems to be one of organic communal harmony. It is a resolution at once psychological and religious: the Mariner shows he is both healed and forgiven by worshipping at peace and harmony with his fellows. Yet if what we are witnessing is some kind of spiritual growth towards personal integration, the logic of this development is, to say the least, obscure. The events of the narrative are arbitrary and magical

[1] 31 May 1830, in *Table Talk*, ed. H. N. Coleridge (London 1852), 86.
[2] 'The Theme of "The Ancient Mariner"', *Scrutiny*, 9 (1941), 341.

rather than 'moral'. The Mariner shoots the albatross for no reason
whatsoever. His fellow sailors are at first horrified, and then, when the
weather improves, praise him for his action. For this inconstancy or error
of judgement they are condemned to die a lingering death. We meet the
spectre bark with its nightmare crew of Death and Life-in-Death. Are
these external figures or symbolic hallucinations? Do they have any
moral significance? If so, what? Most important of all, the Mariner's
release comes with apparent arbitrariness when he is least expecting it:

> Beyond the shadow of the ship,
> I watch'd the water-snakes:
> They mov'd in tracks of shining white;
> And when they rear'd, the elfish light
> Fell off in hoary flakes.
>
> Within the shadow of the ship
> I watch'd their rich attire:
> Blue, glossy green, and velvet black
> They coil'd and swam; and every track
> Was a flash of golden fire.
>
> O happy living things! no tongue
> Their beauty might declare;
> A spring of love gusht from my heart,
> And I bless'd them unaware!
> Sure my kind saint took pity on me,
> And I bless'd them unaware.
>
> The self-same moment I could pray;
> And from my neck so free
> The Albatross fell off, and sank
> Like lead into the sea.   (ll. 269–83)

This is one of those climaxes in which great Romantic art seems to
specialize. One thinks of the last movement of Beethoven's Ninth
Symphony when, after themes and variations from earlier parts have
been tried and found wanting, the amazing final theme that is to be taken
up by the choir a few moments later bursts up, as it were, through those
fragments of earlier and discarded efforts. All that conscious effort that
went before turns out to have been futile—and yet in some mysterious
way *necessary*, since it is only in failure that this sudden uprush of
inspiration occurs. So here in 'The Ancient Mariner' this moment of
liberation is preceded by complete despair: 'Seven days, seven nights, I

saw that curse, / And yet I could not die! (ll. 253–4). Yet, unexpectedly, at this point the Mariner through despair begins to forget himself, and begins to look around him at Nature. Previously even the sea had seemed to mirror the horror of his situation, but now, in the beauty of the moonlight, and when he least expects it, he notices the water-snakes (apparently those same 'slimy' things that he had first reacted to with such loathing) and finds them beautiful. Something in his unconscious is liberated—'a spring of love' gushes from him and he finds he has blessed them 'unaware'.

Clearly, what we are watching here is in some sense a psychological crisis. It is as if, in 'blessing' the water-snakes, the Mariner is accepting and even rejoicing in elements of himself which had previously disgusted and repelled him. If we follow this kind of 'psychological' interpretation, as many critics have done, it is not difficult to see the mysterious spirit 'nine fathom deep' as something in his own unconscious which he has offended against or denied—in other words a neurosis. Such an explanation helps us to make sense of the killing of the albatross: we can regard it, for instance, as some kind of compulsive neurotic act—the mark of a psychotic whose conscious and unconscious are deeply at odds. 'The Ancient Mariner' is a happy stamping-ground for psychological symbol-hunters, whether of Freudian or Jungian persuasions.

This 'psychological' approach to the poem is greatly strengthened by the work of John Livingstone Lowes, one of the finest Coleridge scholars of all time. His book, *The Road to Xanadu*, is a classic of detective brilliance, and any one who really wishes to study 'The Ancient Mariner' or 'Kubla Khan' should read it in full. From Coleridge's notebooks Lowes has patiently followed his reading through the winter and spring of 1797–8 when he was at work on the poem, and demonstrates how much of what he was reading finds its way into it. Coleridge, for instance, had been making notes from Priestley's *Opticks* (a contemporary scientific textbook); he had been reading the letters of a Jesuit missionary from the Pacific, Father Bourzes; as well as the *Voyages* of Captain Cook, and Bartram's *Travels*. Words and phrases from these, and scores of other books, re-emerge in new settings in the poem. Bourzes, for instance, describes fish in the Pacific that leave behind them 'a luminous track' . . . which have made a kind of artificial fire', and Lowes is able to show that Coleridge was making notes from this very page while writing 'The Ancient Mariner'.[3] Line after line of the poem is painstakingly broken down by Lowes' researches into a kind of mosaic of Coleridge's reading—reassembled and transformed by his poetic creativity. Even the

[3] Lowes, *The Road to Xanadu*, 40.

strange and blatantly impossible 'hornéd Moon, with one bright star / Within the nether tip' is run to earth in the *Transactions of the Royal Society*. What we have already seen was going on at one level in the creation of the narrative of the poem by Wordsworth and Coleridge was repeated at another level by Coleridge in the detailed construction of nearly every line and phrase.

We owe Lowes an enormous debt for showing us *how* Coleridge's mind worked as he created a poem. But revealing as this kind of research is, it does not help us much in trying to unravel the *meaning* of the poem. Is the poem, perhaps, no more than its sources: Wordsworth's reading of Shelvock, Priestley, Bourzes, Cook, Bartram, and all the rest? Were Southey and those other first reviewers right in concluding that it *has* no meaning—that it is just an undigested metaphysical mess? This kind of 'psychological' explanation is reductionism run wild: it seeks to explain a work of art in terms of the artist's materials. It ignores the fascination which the poem has exerted on millions of readers over the past two centuries. Are the critics I have been describing earlier right in seeing the poem as about the interpretation of the personality? As the reader may have guessed, I am sceptical. For one thing, it is not clear, as we have seen, that the Mariner *is* healed. Why does the Wedding Guest go like 'one that hath been stunned' and rise 'a sadder and a wiser man' if the message of the poem is psychic integration? Moreover, the blessing of the water-snakes is described in language that is unequivocally religious:

> Sure my kind saint took pity on me
> And I bless'd them unawares.
>
> The self-same moment I could pray. . . .   (ll. 278–80)

This is not the language of psychic growth, but of Christian Grace. The whole framework is that of good and evil, guilt and expiation: 'the man hath penance done / And penance more will do.' And here we come back full circle. The simple Christian message that God loves all his creatures does not satisfy a reading of the poem either.

We seem to be left with a very strange story: one that can be accounted for neither as a Christian parable of sin and redemption, nor as a drama of psychological breakdown and recovery. Indeed, the more we start to look at the psychological level the more it seems to demand some kind of religious explanation, but the more we look at the religious level the more we seem to be forced back again towards some kind of psychological one. Neither seems to be satisfactory without the other—yet they remain, to some degree, mutually exclusive. It seems to move in the borderlands where psychology and religion touch, but where the normal rules, as we understand them, no longer hold good. Yet this challenge to simple clear-cut notions of morality, for all its ambiguity, can be seen as profoundly 'realistic'. Christianity has never claimed that we live in a 'just' universe. The Mariner's motiveless malignancy has, it seems to me, the same quality of psychological realism that we find in Wordsworth's 'Nutting'—and the incident of the shooting was, we recall, originally suggested by Wordsworth. Such a 'realism' is not inconsistent with a symbolic landscape. The spectre bark, with its nightmare crew of Death and Life-in-Death actually has its origins in the dream of a friend of Coleridge's, John Cruikshank, who lived in Nether Stowey. If we compare the world of 'The Ancient Mariner' to that of a dream, it is not in the sense the Victorian critics were quick to use it, that of an 'escapist' or unreal world, but with our modern recognition of the reality and significance of dreams as a clue to our own deepest experiences. Clearly the vision of the ghostly ship is part of the Mariner's punishment, but it merely describes his condition without any attempt at justice or morality. As in our own deepest fantasies, we cannot separate choice from arbitrary event—and it is significant that neither do the basic Christian myths, such as the story of the Fall itself. We do not live in a world that is governed by our choice, just as we do not live in a world that is without choice. Coleridge and Wordsworth had originally planned to write a poem about another figure beloved of Romantic mythology, the Wandering Jew. It is as if the Mariner at the Wedding Feast is the Jew. At the moment of festivity and thanksgiving, the unthinking guest is suddenly and irresistibly confronted with a story of mysterious guilt and suffering—a reminder that the cosy world of rationality that we insist is 'normal' stands perched on the edge of an abyss.

If the balance is a precarious one, we need to remind ourselves that that is, in part, the *meaning* of the poem. We also need to remind ourselves that this is an echo, at another level, of what the *Lyrical Ballads* are attempting as a whole. I said at the beginning that the sheer familiarity of 'The Ancient Mariner' can prevent us from seeing its continuity with the other 1798 *Ballads*. Wordsworth's poetry, superficially very different in kind, spans a range from the simple and magical tale of 'Goody Blake and Harry Gill' to the much deeper visionary and psychological explorations of 'Tintern Abbey', but in its totality it encompasses a comparable moral complexity. We need to see the 'realism' of 'The Ancient Mariner' in this context of joint creation by Wordsworth and Coleridge. As the opening poem of the first edition of the *Ballads* it is, in two senses, the *way into* their unique achievement of 1798.

Simon Lee, Anecdote for Fathers, We Are Seven

One of the reasons why Wordsworth is so demanding on the attention of the reader is his apparent simplicity. Over and over again in the *Lyrical Ballads* we find him attempting to capture a point of the most complex psychology within a form that is simple almost to the point of naïvety. Nor are we going to come to grips with the difficulty of Wordsworth as a poet unless we see how essential to his purposes this superficial simplicity is.

Perhaps his throw-away technique reaches its epitome in 'Simon Lee'.

> O reader! had you in your mind
> Such stores as silent thought can bring,
> O gentle reader! you would find
> A tale in every thing.
> What more I have to say is short,
> I hope you'll kindly take it;
> It is no tale; but should you think,
> Perhaps a tale you'll make it.   (ll. 73–80)

Poetically, this is Wordsworth at his worst. But it is at moments like this, when his technique is at its most threadbare, that we can often see most clearly what he is trying to do. He is deliberately turning his back on the 'story' in favour of the single incident—what in *The Prelude* (where he does it successfully) he called a 'spot of time'. The single moment of insight carries a significance far wider than itself, giving meaning and shape to whole areas of human experience. Wordsworth saw his own growth in terms of a succession of such 'spots of time'. As the last lines tell us, 'Simon Lee', of course, is about gratitude. Godwin, the philosopher from whose theories Wordsworth had only just succeeded in extricating himself with the help of Coleridge and Dorothy, argued that 'if by gratitude we understand a sentiment of preference which I entertain towards another, upon the ground of my having been the subject of his benefits, it is no part of justice or virtue'.[4] Wordsworth is determined to show this up for the over-sophisticated nonsense he believed it to be. His reply is not a story, but simply the description of a moment of gratitude. Rural life depended not merely on reciprocity of services rendered by neighbours, but on the spirit that goes beyond any calculation of advantages. Generosity and gratitude are a part of the proper dignity of human life; they are not conventions of society for the smooth-running of its machinery but ends and values in themselves. Urban life may make

[4] *Lyrical Ballads*, 284.

this sometimes hard to see, but in simple rural life it is still unmistakable. Wordsworth in his poetry conducts a constant fight against 'reductionism' in all its forms. 'Gratitude' is not 'nothing but' a 'preference' for those who have helped us. Human feeling is not an extra—a way of making the boredom of the rich interesting and the toil of the poor tolerable—but what gives meaning to social relationships.

But emotions are not simple or easy to explain rationally. Godwin's 'behaviourism', Wordsworth believed, was also wrong on this point. Like Wordsworth, Godwin believed in the fundamental innocence of childhood, and he argued from this that lying is not natural to children but is the product of an evil social system. In an 'Anecdote for Fathers' Wordsworth outflanks Godwin by means of a simple parable. With nice irony, the child in question, 'little Edward', is the son of Basil Montague, an old friend of Wordsworth, who was himself an enthusiastic Godwinian. The little boy had gone to live with the Wordsworths at Racedown after his mother had died, and, according to Wordsworth, he used to lie 'like a little devil'.[5] As he so often does in the geography of his poems, Wordsworth has invented a fictional landscape by taking names from different parts of the country: Kilve *is* on the coast only a short distance from Alfoxden, but Liswyn Farm is probably 'Lyswen', the Brecknockshire home of their revolutionary friend Thelwall, who was also an ardent Godwinian.

Every word of the deceptively casual setting is important. The natural instinctive (Godwinian) innocence of the boy is given visual form with his 'fair and fresh' complexion, and the pastoral scenery and 'rustic dress' reinforce with literary convention the picture of simple virtue. The conversation that ensues is, to begin with, quite unforced. He talks to the little boy 'in very idleness' and the boy replies 'in careless mood'. The gap between the child's view of the world and his elder's is not apparent until, suddenly, the adult tries to press him to give a *reason* for his preference.

> Now, little Edward, say why so;
> My little Edward, tell me why;   (ll. 37–8)

The point is worthy of Piaget or Spock. His intention, said Wordsworth afterwards, was 'to point out the injurious effects of putting inconsiderate questions to Children, and urging them to give answers upon matters either uninteresting to them, or upon which they have no decided

[5] Wordsworth to Francis Wrangham, 7 March 1796, in *Letters, Early Years* (2nd edn), 168.

opinion'.[6] It is a source of never-failing fascination to see how often a small child, when asked, 'What did you do in school today?' will reply 'nothing'—when later he is found to be bursting to tell his parents about some event of great importance in his life. Below a certain age, it is as if the insistent questioning of an adult dries up a child's powers of reply. A child speaks in his own time, and cannot be forced to another's. So here, the ingenious Edward fastens upon an obvious lie to silence the grown-up intruder.

The simplicity of the poem. with its four-line rhyming stanzas and insistent repetition of key phrases is not the simplicity of the ballad—where a similar technique is used to a quite different end. 'Anecdote for Fathers' is a parable. Its structure is more like that of a modern short story where the key is hinted at, but left unsaid—a *What Maisie Knew* in verse. The motives and reasoning may be complicated and obscure, but these are best explored by giving us only the bare bones and demanding our response to flesh them out. The technique depends upon the contrast between the naïvety of the narration and the unspoken complexity it implies. The effect is in many ways the direct opposite of Coleridge's, and it is one that Wordsworth was repeatedly to strive for in the *Lyrical Ballads*, using it in some of his most successful poems—perhaps most notably in 'We Are Seven', a poem to which Coleridge contributed the opening stanza.

Though 'We Are Seven' again depends on the contrast and even tension between the 'naïve' vision of the child and the unspoken sophistication of the adult reader, whereas in an 'Anecdote for Fathers' the understanding of the adult is necessary in the poem to interpret the 'lies' of the child and so lead to a moment of sudden revelation, here the irony is directed against the adult—who remains unenlightened. It is the simple childish vision which is valuable, and the adult's superior 'wisdom' which inhibits insight. The point of course is not that the child is instinctively 'religious' in the conventional sense: it is the adult who insists piously that 'Their spirits are in Heaven'. For the child, there *is* no division. The adult can only recapture this vision of unity through the kind of complex sophistication we find Wordsworth exploring in the 'Lucy' poems which appeared in the second volume of the *Ballads* in 1800.

> A slumber did my spirit seal,
> I had no human fears:
> She seem'd a thing that could not feel
> The touch of earthly years.

[6] *Letters, Later Years* (1st edn), I, 253.

> No motion has she now, no force;
> She neither hears nor sees;
> Roll'd round in earth's diurnal course,
> With rocks, and stones, and trees.

Here the unity of the living and the dead is presented in a much more disturbing and ambiguous light. A. P. Rossiter has called attention to the change of tense between the two stanzas.[7] The effect of this is to enable us to read the poem in two quite different ways. If the first stanza describes the period in the past when 'Lucy' was alive, what he seems to be saying is that during that time he was caught up in an almost trance-like state of bliss when his loved one seemed immune from the touch and change of time. In contrast, the second stanza recalls him to the present when she is dead—her one-time vitality absorbed into the cold inanimate earth. Read in this way, the poem seems to reflect a physical horror of death. If, on the other hand, we take the first stanza to be describing not a period of time but a single visionary instant after the death of his beloved, then the second stanza is what he saw then—and believes to be permanently true. In her grave she has become united with Nature as never before, and has even achieved a kind of mute but peaceful immortality. Clearly, read in this way the poem is resigned, or even hopeful in tone. Which interpretation are we to take? Wordsworth gives us no clue—perhaps for the very good reason that he himself was not sure. In other words, the poem is not about the resolution of the problem of death for Wordsworth, but is about the *problem* itself. For all the apparent contradiction between the two readings, once we have seen them both we cannot then completely obliterate either—leaving us in a condition of what Empson calls 'radical indecision'.[8] Wordsworth is a poet, not a metaphysician, and the advantage of poetry is that it enables the writer to put side by side two opposite and contradictory states of mind and hold them, as it were, in suspension. His poetry, as the *Lyrical Ballads* illustrate, has a constant tendency to move from its ostensible object to a consideration of his own state of mind. Writing a poem was, for Wordsworth, an act of self-exploration.

The Female Vagrant, The Last of the Flock

But the unity of life that is one of the insistent themes of the *Lyrical*

---

[7] This brief outline cannot do justice to Rossiter's subtle discussion of ambiguity in this poem. See 'Ambivalence: The Dialectic of the Histories', in *Angel with Horns* (London 1961), 48.

[8] *Seven Types of Ambiguity* (2nd edn, Peregrine, Harmondsworth 1961).

Ballads cannot be confined to parables on psychology—whether of the poet's own state of mind, or of others'. Wordsworth and Coleridge's poetical radicalism *could* only go hand-in-hand with political radicalism. Coleridge, with *The Watchman*, had been for a time an effective political journalist; Wordsworth's commitment to the ideals of the French Revolution had been total, and in 1794 he had written a powerful attack on the institution of the monarchy, the aristocracy, and the prevalent economic system in his 'Letter to the Bishop of Llandaff'.[9] In his own day Wordsworth was as often picked out as the poet of the poor as he was the poet of Nature.[10] It is in this tradition of uncompromising political radicalism that we must see two of Wordsworth's best poems of the *Lyrical Ballads*, 'The Female Vagrant' and 'The Last of the Flock'.

The history of the text of 'The Female Vagrant' is the story of the decline and fall of Wordsworth's revolutionary ideals. As the poem appears in the first edition of the *Lyrical Ballads* it is an outspoken attack on wealthy landowners, war, and the whole fabric of a social system that used the poor to fight for the privileges of the rich. Later it was incorporated, with numerous revisions, into a much larger poem called 'Salisbury Plain', and later still its title was changed to 'Guilt and Sorrow.'[11] Each revision progressively tones down the note of social protest, so central to this first version:

> The suns of twenty summers danced along,—
> Ah! little marked, how fast they rolled away:
> Then rose a mansion proud our woods among,
> And cottage after cottage owned its sway,
> No joy to see a neighbouring house, or stray
> Through pastures not his own, the master took;
> My Father dared his greedy wish gainsay;
> He loved his old hereditary nook,
> And ill could I the thought of such sad parting brook.
>
> But, when he had refused the proffered gold,
> To cruel injuries he became a prey,
> Sore traversed in whate'er he bought and sold.
> His troubles grew upon him day by day,

[9] Moorman, I, 225–9.

[10] Strikingly noticeable, for instance, in Keble's Crewian Oration to Wordsworth when he was given an honorary degree by Oxford University in 1839.

[11] For a fuller account of this complicated textual history see *Poetical Works*, ed. E. de Selincourt, I, 330–4, I, xvi, 292–5.

> Till all his substance fell into decay.
> His little range of water was denied;
> All but the bed where his old body lay,
> All, all was seized, and weeping, side by side,
> We sought a home where we uninjured might abide.
>
> (ll. 37–54)

Wordsworth is not merely protesting against the effects of the enclosure movement—which strengthened the rich and often, as here, deprived the small man of what little he possessed—he is also attacking the attitude of mind of the new landowners. The owner of the mansion takes 'no joy to see a neighbouring house'. As we have seen in the case of 'Simon Lee', Wordsworth's experience of rural society (and especially his native Cumberland people) had led him to feel how all-important were the basic communal virtues of generosity, honesty, dignity and respect for individuals. A man who was 'un-neighbourly' cut against the very foundations of society. The pride of the rich who wished to have an uninterrupted view was a crime equivalent to the Mariner's against the order of Nature.

In the final version of 'The Female Vagrant', however, all this is omitted, and we find merely the vague statement: 'But through severe mischance and cruel wrong / My father's substance fell into decay.'

There is a parallel retreat in the description of the soldiers. In the 1798 version their misery is seen as yet another form of the all-pervading political oppression of the poor by the rich:

> Oh! dreadful price of being to resign
> All that is dear *in* being! better far . . .
> . . . in the streets and walks where proud men are,
> Better our dying bodies to obtrude,
> Than dog-like, wading at the heels of war,
> Protract a curst existence, with the brood
> That lap (their very nourishment!) their brother's blood.
>
> (ll. 118–26)

As early as the 1802 edition of the *Lyrical Ballads* these lines had been excised, yet without them much of the irony of what follows is lost on the reader.

> The pains and plagues that on our heads came down,
> Disease and famine, agony and fear,
> In wood or wilderness, in camp or town,

> It would thy brain unsettle even to hear.
> All perished—all, in one remorseless year,
> Husband and children! one by one, by sword
> And ravenous plague, all perished; every tear
> Dried up, despairing, desolate, on board
> A British ship I waked, as from a trance restored.
>
> (ll. 127–35)

It is patriotism that gives Wordsworth's sense of outraged justice such a
biting edge. He is angry not simply at the 'pity of war', but at the pity
that the families and dependants of British soldiers should be so cast aside
by their own countrymen. Dorothy's *Journal*, kept as a day-to-day record
of the Wordsworths' life at Grasmere where they moved in 1800, is full of
reference to vagrants—the flotsam and jetsam of the continuing wars
with France who had served their purpose and were now abandoned to
wander the roads of the mother country who had no longer any use for
the crippled or bereaved.

Outraged patriotism is similarly the keynote to the even more
outspokenly political 'The Last of the Flock':

> In distant countries I have been,
> And yet I have not often seen
> A healthy man, a man full grown
> Weep in the public roads alone.
> But such a one, on English ground,
> And in the broad high-way, I met;
> Along the broad high-way he came,
> His cheeks with tears were wet.
> Sturdy he seemed, though he was sad;
> And in his arms a lamb he had.

The poem is based upon an incident that had happened in Holford, close
by Wordsworth's Quantock home at Alfoxden, and it is important for
him that the story is actually *true*. The female vagrant's downfall is
representative of many who had lost their place in society, but as a
representative story the details, even in the earliest version, remain vague.
But this tragedy, is a factual narrative 'on English ground' (however
representative of other cases) and the shame of its being English and that it
could happen so publicly on an English high-road strengthens
Wordsworth's patriotic disgust. The particular story is, nevertheless,
peculiarly representative of two evils Wordsworth had come to abhor.
At a social level it epitomized a system of poor relief that denied assistance

to the small man until it was too late, forcing him to sell all his property before he could receive temporary assistance.

> 'I of the parish ask'd relief.
> They said I was a wealthy man;
> My sheep upon the mountain fed,
> And it was fit that thence I took
> Whereof to buy us bread;'
> 'Do this; how can we give to you,'
> They cried, 'what to the poor is due?'

Thus the thrifty and hardworking were pauperized to the same degree as the idle and shiftless. Assistance came in such a form as to prevent him from ever recovering independence. Wordsworth again takes up the cudgels for the small man—the independent poor who were squeezed between the upper and the nether millstones of a society in rapid and painful economic change. The rich, when beset by temporary difficulty—what we now call 'liquidity problems'—could always borrow; the poor could not. Thus the apparently iron laws of Malthus, that the population expanded to the point where it was checked by misery, were invisibly upheld by a system which made his gloomiest predictions certain to be true. On the face of it, this story appears to be a Malthusian parable—illustrating the evils of too many children—but Wordsworth was not worried about the dangers of over-population. Malthus published his *Essay on Population* in 1798, the same year as the *Lyrical Ballads*, and both he and Wordsworth are responding to one of the greatest social questions of the day: what to do about the growing numbers of destitute and poor who were becoming an impossible burden on the parish rates. Needless to say, Wordsworth would have no truck with the view that poverty and misery were necessary and inevitable. But behind his attack on the prevalent system of outdoor parish relief, which in the long run actually cost more by its pauperizing tactics, Wordsworth is making a more important philosophical point. Godwin had argued that private property was the root of all evil. Growing up in the Lake District Wordsworth had experienced an upbringing of peculiar egalitarianism, and his strong boyhood sense of the dignity of 'Cumberland democracy' never deserted him:

> . . . born in a poor district, and which yet
> Retaineth more of ancient homeliness,
> Manners erect, and frank simplicity,
> Than any other nook of English land,

> It was my fortune scarcely to have seen
> Through the whole tenor of my school-day time
> The face of one, who, whether boy or man,
> Was vested with attention or respect
> Through claims of wealth or blood; . . .
>
> > (*Prelude* 1805, IX, ll. 217–25)

But if property conferred no status in the eyes of the sturdy Cumberland 'statesmen', as the small farmers were called, it did confer the financial independence that made this freedom of the spirit possible. As Legouis comments, 'The man who holds with Godwin that property is the cause of every vice and the source of all the misery of the poor is naturally astonished to find that this so-called evil, the offspring of human institutions, is a vigorous instinct closely interwoven with the noblest feelings. It represents familiar and dearly-loved fields, a hereditary cottage, and flocks every animal of which has its own name.'[12]

The Brothers, Michael

This interaction of feeling for place, for land, and for people as indivisible aspects of a single unity is presented by Wordsworth at its strongest in two poems that he included in the second volume of the 1800 *Ballads*—'The Brothers' and 'Michael'. Neither is an easy poem for modern readers, in that passive endurance and stoicism are not qualities instantly commanding respect today. We who are reared on newspaper 'tragedies' are not as deeply moved as Wordsworth's own age by 'affecting' tales of sentiment. Wordsworth is using a popular genre for his own purposes, but the genre itself has fallen victim to a shift in sensibility. Yet both poems are essential for understanding Wordsworth's sense of the dignity of stoical suffering, and of the depth of feeling concealed by the restraint of those living and working in contact with the elemental forms of Nature. We recall his lines in *The Borderers*:

> Action is transitory . . .
> Suffering is permanent, obscure and dark,
> And shares the nature of infinity.

Two of Wordsworth's own children were to be buried in Grasmere churchyard in the next few years.

Expostulation and Reply; The Tables Turned

For Wordsworth, the poet was concerned with the *whole* man, in all his

---

[12] Emile Legouis, *The Early Life of Wordsworth*, 310.

social and economic relationships, and not with fragments, disfigured and dismembered by literary convention, social system, or *a priori* political philosophy. It is for this reason that Wordsworth attacks Godwin over and over again with all the vehemence of an ex-disciple, even while remaining on relatively good terms with him personally. As a thinker, Godwin often seems to epitomize for Wordsworth all the harshness, the shallowness, and reductionism of an intelligence that has become severed from feeling. Wordsworth came to distrust the rootless intellect as one of the most dangerous and potentially destructive of all human perversions. This is the underlying assumption behind two of his best—but most difficult—poems in the *Lyrical Ballads*—'Expostulation and Reply' and 'The Tables Turned'. The philosopher forgets the unity of human experience at his peril:

> The eye it cannot chuse but see,
> We cannot bid the ear be still;
> Our bodies feel, where'er they be,
> Against, or with our will.
>
> Nor less I deem that there are powers,
> Which of themselves our minds impress,
> That we can feed this mind of ours,
> In a wise passiveness.   ('E. & R.', ll. 17–24)

Wordsworth's psychology, at this period, like Coleridge's follows Hartley. The great strength of his system in their eyes was that it was able to suggest a physical and therefore 'scientific' basis for this unity of the personality. For Hartley, the mind itself is nothing more than a totally passive 'sensorium' which contains 'ideas' in the form of a mass of minute vibrations in the nervous system (or, as he calls them, 'vibratiuncles'). New sensations of sight, sound, etc., 'which of themselves our minds impress', come as vibrations to a mind which is itself the legacy of all past sensations. Each individual has therefore his own personal and unique pattern of vibrations which will modify succeeding ones in its own unique way—just as the infinitely variable ground-swell of the ocean will affect the ripple-pattern of a pebble thrown into it. Thus the way in which each person perceives the world will be conditioned by the total previous history of his mind up to that point. For Hartley, the growth of the mind was accomplished in a series of seven inevitable stages of increasing complexity, beginning with simple sensation and ending with Moral Sense.[13] It is easy to see why, at first sight, Hartley seemed to

[13] For a fuller account of the influence of Hartley on Wordsworth and Coleridge, see my *Coleridge and Wordsworth: The Poetry of Growth*, 46–70.

provide the very theory of development that Wordsworth and Coleridge needed: so great was Coleridge's admiration for the philosopher at this time that he named his eldest son after him. By the early 1800s, however, he had turned violently against Hartley as he came to realize that a passive and mechanical system of psychology negated the very powers that he so passionately believed in. Wordsworth's Hartleian phase seems to have outlasted Coleridge's, and it is likely that this philosophical disagreement was yet another reason for Wordsworth assuming greater responsibility for the 'manifesto' aspects of the *Lyrical Ballads*.

Here, in 'Expostulation and Reply', the 'wise passiveness' of a heart that 'watches and receives' is that which receives from Nature the sensations for a healthy moral and spiritual development. 'Passivity' and contemplation are in line with the very physical processes of Nature herself:

> Sweet is the lore which nature brings;
> Our meddling intellect
> Mishapes the beauteous forms of things;
> —We murder to dissect.
>
> Enough of science and of Art;
> Close up these barren leaves;
> Come forth, and bring with you a heart
> That watches and receives.   ('T.T.', ll. 25–8)

To understand what Wordsworth means by this we cannot do better than turn to an account he wrote of the development of a boy's mind, nearly ten years later, in his excellent and little-read 'Letter to Mathetes'. It was published as a contribution to Coleridge's periodical, *The Friend*, in January 1810. Two Scots, John Wilson and Alexander Blair had written to Coleridge under the pen-name of 'Mathetes' to ask whether he thought that any child of genius could survive the educational system of the day. Coleridge gave the job of replying to Wordsworth, who answers by arguing that we underrate the strength and resilience of youth (whether genius or not) under even the most difficult conditions.

Significantly, Wordsworth sees the development of manhood beginning in the boy's willingness to come to terms with past failures. Their memory must not be suppressed, but rather accepted and understood.

> . . . he cannot recall past time; he cannot begin his journey afresh; he cannot untwist the links by which, in no undelightful harmony, images and sentiments are wedded in his mind. Granted that the sacred

light of Childhood is and must be for him no more than a remembrance. He may, notwithstanding, be remanded to Nature; and with trust-worthy hopes; founded less upon his sentient than upon his intellectual Being—to Nature, not as leading on insensibly to the Society of Reason; but to Reason and Will as leading back to the wisdom of Nature . . . the two powers of Reason and Nature, thus reciprocally teacher and taught, may advance together in a track to which there is no limit.[14]

'Nature' and 'Reason' are not opposed to each other, but go properly hand in hand. Wordsworth's beliefs have not changed in the ten years since the *Lyrical Ballads*. The key is what he elsewhere calls 'Feeling'—not a matter of primitive passion, or blind irrational emotion, but something which grows only very slowly with the whole person, and which includes the intellectual capacities. The 'wise passiveness' of the heart 'that watches and receives' is not a vegetable complacency, but rather the activity of 'Reason' which is the very antithesis of the deracinated 'meddling intellect'; it involves a consciousness of self as a unity, and a consciousness of man's interdependence with the natural world. Wordsworth goes on to illustrate his argument with a very revealing image:

There never perhaps existed a School-boy who, having when he retired to rest, carelessly blown out his candle, and having chanced to notice as he lay upon his bed in the ensuing darkness, the sullen light which had survived the extinguished flame, did not, at some time or other, watch that light as if his mind were bound to it by a spell. It fades and revives—gathers to a point—seems as if it would go out in a moment—again recovers its strength, nay becomes brighter than before: it continues to shine with an endurance, which in its apparent weakness is a mystery—it protracts its existence so long, clinging to the power which supports it, that the Observer, who had laid down in his bed so easy-minded, becomes sad and melancholy: his sympathies are touched—it is to him an intimation and an image of departing human life. . . . This is Nature teaching seriously and sweetly through the affections—melting the heart, and, through that instinct of tenderness, developing the understanding. . . .[15]

The passage is an important one, and worth quoting at some length since it makes explicit the attitude to 'Nature' that runs throughout his work.

[14] *The Friend*, ed. B. E. Rooke, (London 1969), II, 263.
[15] *Ibid.*, 264.

There is no intrinsic importance in the event or object itself in this illustration—it is merely the dying spark on a wick. The significance lies in its symbolic value to the mind that contemplates it. Nature's 'teaching', we notice, is not to be found in the glowing candle-end alone but in the imaginative response of the boy as well. It consists of an interaction of external stimulus (in itself trivial) and internal response. Its value is to be found not merely in the reflections it triggers off at the time, but, even more, in the memory of those reflections afterwards—the 'emotion recollected in tranquillity'. What was essentially a slight incident has become a point of growth and spiritual nourishment:

> . . . the image of the dying taper may be recalled and contemplated, though with no sadness in the nerves, no disposition to tears, no unconquerable sighs. . . . Let then the Youth go back, as occasion will permit, to Nature and to Solitude, thus admonished by Reason, and relying upon this newly-acquired support. A world of fresh sensations will gradually open upon him as his mind puts off its infirmities, and . . . he makes it his prime business to understand himself.[16]

Wordsworth's account of the growing boy is clearly auto-biographical—though he believes his own experiences are of wider significance, his starting-point is the poet's mind. The development of the artist is the development of Everyman, as it were, writ large. It is this balance of emotion and intellect that Wordsworth finds in Nature's teaching through the imagination that he finds so lacking in ordinary so-called education. 'One impulse from a vernal wood' is of such importance precisely because it is not an impulse in isolation, but is part of a process of growth and imaginative development. To see this process at work more fully, in a heart 'that watches and receives', we must turn now to Wordsworth's greatest single contribution to the *Lyrical Ballads*. By another of those happy accidents that characterize the first edition, 'Tintern Abbey' concludes the volume, and completes what 'The Ancient Mariner' began.

Tintern Abbey

'Tintern Abbey' was not intended to be part of the *Lyrical Ballads* at all. The other poems were already at the printers when William and Dorothy went on a walking-tour of the Wye valley in July 1798. It was written at great speed, and, unlike most of Wordsworth's poems, it was not revised or altered afterwards. 'No poem of mine,' wrote Wordsworth afterwards, 'was composed under circumstances more

[16] *Ibid.*, 264.

pleasant for me to remember than this. I began it upon leaving Tintern, after crossing the Wye, and concluded it just as I was entering Bristol in the evening, after a ramble of four or five days, with my sister. Not a line of it was altered, and not any part of it was written down till I reached Bristol.'[17]

It is a poem about an anniversary. Though one might not guess so from the deceptive peace of the opening lines, Wordsworth is revisiting the scene of the greatest crisis of his life. The very peace of the scene is part of the contrast between then, five years before, and now, when he stands again beneath the same dark sycamore tree. Five years takes us back to the summer of 1793 when Wordsworth came on his own to Tintern. He had originally set out with his friend Raisley Calvert for a 'Tour of the West', but while crossing Salisbury Plain they had suffered an accident and their 'whiskey' (a kind of one-horse trap) was overturned and smashed. Calvert took his horse and went home, leaving Wordsworth to push on towards Wales on foot. Probably there was more than the accident behind the separation. Wordsworth was in a state of deep depression—perhaps even feeling suicidal. His whole life seemed to be in ruins. His early enthusiasm for the ideals of the French Revolution had been dashed by its inexorable movement towards tyranny and terror. With many of his friends dead or in exile, he had returned to England penniless and disillusioned. To his patriotic shame, England was now at war with the revolutionary France. Moreover, he had other, personal, reasons for despair. While in France he had fallen in love with a French girl of a good family called Annette Vallon. Her parents, Catholic and royalist, opposed the idea of marriage with this Protestant English revolutionary sympathizer—and there is no doubt that his family, had they known, would also have opposed the match. In a deliberate effort to force the family's consent, Annette became pregnant. The plan went dramatically awry. Annette was removed by her furious family, and Wordsworth was prevented from seeing her—and the child that was born in December 1792. Returning to England in 1793 Wordsworth was leaving not merely his hopes for the regeneration of mankind, but the girl he loved and an illegitimate child he had never seen.

This, then, is the background to the peace and serenity of the opening of 'Tintern Abbey'. What had happened in the intervening five years to work the transformation of mood? The description of the valley (much of it, incidentally, paraphrased from their guide-book, Gilpin's *Tour of the Wye*) is the setting for the description of Wordsworth's inner life that follows.'These forms of beauty' have been to him a comfort and a solace,

[17] *Lyrical Ballads*, 296.

and, more, the key to a joy that has given meaning to the darkest points in
his life.

> ——that serene and blessed mood,
> In which the affections gently lead us on,——
> Until, the breath of this corporeal frame,
> And even the motion of our human blood
> Almost suspended, we are laid asleep
> In body, and become a living soul:
> While with an eye made quiet by the power
> Of harmony, and the deep power of joy,
> We see into the life of things.   (ll. 42–50)

It is clear that Wordsworth is describing something much more than a
mere feeling of happiness connected with his memories of Nature and
their healing powers. Is this a description of some kind of mystical
experience—was Wordsworth a 'mystic'? It all depends, of course, on
what we mean by the word. Coleridge, much later in his life, defined it
like this:

> When a man refers to *inward feelings* and *experiences*, of which
> mankind at large are not conscious, as evidences of the truth of any
> opinion—such as Man I call a MYSTIC: and the grounding of any
> theory or belief on accidents and anomalies of individual sensations or
> fancies, and the use of peculiar terms invented or perverted from their
> ordinary signification, for the purposes of expressing these
> idiosyncrasies, and pretended facts of interior consciousness, I name
> MYSTICISM. . . .[18]

Clearly Wordsworth was not a 'mystic' in this kind of sense. Though he
sometimes describes *unusual* experiences, they are never claimed as
exclusive—things of which mankind in general is not conscious.
Wordsworth always believed that potentially, at any rate, these
experiences were open to anyone. The poet, as we have said, was in his
view not a different kind of man, but a representative man.

'The blessed mood' seems to be the product of these memories of
beauty on his poetic creativity: the process of 'emotion recollected in
tranquillity'. But here it seems to have achieved a new and special status
of peculiar intensity. The important word is 'joy':

> . . . with an eye made quiet by the power
> Of harmony, and the deep power of joy
> We see into the life of things.

[18] *Aids to Reflection*, Edinburgh 1905, 349.

When Wordsworth talks of 'joy' in this way we find, very often, that it is associated with two other kinds of experience. The first is that of failure, fear, and despair—moments that are apparently the very antithesis of joy. Near the end of *The Prelude*, for example, he tells us how as a child he came upon a place where there had once been a gibbet where a murderer had been hanged. On the turf someone had cut the murderer's name. The young Wordsworth was terrified—and the memory of it haunted him for years. When, years later, he became engaged to Mary Hutchinson one of his first acts was to take her to see the spot where he had been so frightened. This is what he says:

> When in the blessed time of early love,
> Long afterwards, I roamed about
> In daily presence of this very scene
> Upon the naked pool and dreary crags,
> And on the melancholy beacon, fell
> The spirit of pleasure and youth's golden gleam;
> And think ye not with radiance more divine
> From these remembrances, and from the power
> They left behind?   (1805, XI, ll. 316–26)

It is a very curious notion at first sight. Why should the memory of past fears be such an important element of present happiness, leaving a 'radiance *more* divine'? Wordsworth believed in facing his problems. He never ran away from himself. What gives him joy here, as in 'Tintern Abbey', is the knowledge that he has confronted and overcome his fears, his doubts, and despair. Present strength is based on the memory of past failures. As he argues in the 'Letter to Mathetes', so in 'Tintern Abbey' it is not just *any* 'beauteous forms' that have provided Wordsworth with 'tranquil restoration', but specifically the memory of his despair on that first visit and the knowledge that he has faced and overcome it. The 'joy' in this landscape is the supreme example of 'Nature's teaching'.

But it is no accident that he uses the word 'blessed' to describe his condition in 'Tintern Abbey', or that the parallel passage in *The Prelude* talks of 'radiance divine'. 'Joy' for Wordsworth has specifically religious associations. The Church of England of Wordsworth's own day was lax and corrupt. When the Wordsworths moved to Grasmere in 1800 they very rarely went to church since the curate was usually drunk. It was no place for powerful feelings of any kind. 'Enthusiasm' was a dirty word. Joy was no part of religious experience—and indeed religious experience itself was deeply suspect if it involved violent emotions. But in the middle of the eighteenth century, some fifty years earlier, we find in the poetry of the Methodist revival a new idea appearing: that joy is a part of creativity. For John and Charles Wesley 'joy' was not primarily an attribute of man's at all, but of God—it is the emotion of God in creation. Man's joy came from sharing in his Master's. At the Creation, the Bible tells us, 'the morning stars sang together, and all the sons of God shouted for joy.' From the text in John's Gospel, 'The Word was made flesh, and dwelt among us' (John 1.14) Charles Wesley writes this:

> Transform'd by the ecstatic sight,
> Our souls o'erflow with pure delight,
>   And every moment own
> The Lord our whole perfection is,
> The Lord is our immortal bliss,
> And Christ and heaven are one.[19]

In joy, 'transform'd' man was partaking in an essentially divine activity—and touching the very mystery of creation. Joy *overflows* as it were into creativity. Wordsworth, though he had no Methodist leanings, was probably familiar with this fervent minority tradition of religious experience: his friend and fellow-poet Southey was later to write a biography of Wesley. As for Coleridge in 'Kubla Khan', creation was a *holy* thing.

Thus when Wordsworth in 'Tintern Abbey' turns again to contemplation of the scene before him, he is thinking simultaneously about the process of growth and of poetic creativity: 'That in this moment there is life and food / For future years . . . .' He takes us through his changing and developing attitude to Nature:

>   I cannot paint
> What then I was. The sounding cataract
> Haunted me like a passion: the tall rock,
> The mountain, and the deep and gloomy wood,
> Their colours and their forms, were then to me
> An appetite: a feeling and a love,
> That had no need of a remoter charm,
> By thought supplied, or any interest
> Unborrowed from the eye.—That time is past,
> And all its aching joys are now no more,
> And all its dizzy raptures. Not for this

[19] Charles Wesley, *Short Hymns on Select Passages of the Holy Scriptures*, 1796, II, 202.

> Faint I, nor mourn nor murmur: other gifts
> Have followed, for such loss, I would believe,
> Abundant recompense. For I have learned
> To look on nature, not as in the hour
> Of thoughtless youth, but hearing oftentimes
> The still, sad music of humanity. . . .   (ll. 76–92)

Wordsworth is contrasting two stages of development—then and now. From the way in which he talks of what then he was it is clear that he is thinking of a much wider span of his youth than just his previous visit to Tintern in 1793—even if the description of himself as more like a man 'Flying from something that he dreads than one / Who sought the thing he loved' is applicable to that first visit. If we want a portrait of the instinctive youth with his 'glad animal movements', we can find it in the first two books of *The Prelude*. All this seems to refer back to his boyhood in the Lake District when he was at school in Hawkshead rather than to 1793, when he could certainly not be described as having 'no need of a remoter charm unborrowed from the eye.' If we want a reference to the terrible crisis of 1793, it is more to be found in the 'still, sad music of humanity'—words which are cometimes quoted as a cliché, but which were certainly no cliché for Wordsworth who had come to it the hard way, and for whom the 'sense sublime / Of something far more deeply interfused' was dependent on the more sombre vision of the adult who had come through the experience of breakdown and recovery:

> And I have felt
> A presence that disturbs me with the joy
> Of elevated thoughts; a sense sublime
> Of something far more deeply interfused,
> Whose dwelling is the light of setting suns,
> And the round ocean, and the living air,
> And the blue sky, and in the mind of man,
> A motion and a spirit, that impels
> All thinking things, all objects of all thought,
> And rolls through all things.   (ll. 94–103)

One distinguished critic, William Empson, has scornfully dismissed these lines as 'non-denominational uplift'—a Wordsworthian blur of hurrah-words cloaking some ill-defined, if intensely-felt pantheism, where God is hopefully felt to be present in all beautiful things. Yet Wordsworth is more specific than this gibe suggests. The 'light of setting suns' is certainly beautiful—and we are less than human if we do not value beauty—but for Wordsworth this is only part of the picture. It is not necessary to *prove* God from Nature in order for the believer to see God in Nature. What we are talking about are not matters of proof, but powers of response. The influence of various philosophers, like Newton and Berkeley, and even Spinoza have been detected in the passage.[20] But Wordsworth was not primarily a philosopher—though, like Coleridge, he was well-read in philosophy. He was a poet. The influence of Berkeley, for instance, is to make him feel even more intensely the reality of his sense-perceptions: the round ocean, and the living air, and the blue sky are not just things to be passively looked at; they are to be *felt*, with wonder and excitement. It takes great art to make us see Nature in a new way. Wordsworth had read Newton's *Opticks*. He knew that sense-perception is itself a 'deeply-interfused' relationship between man and his surroundings. Colour is not a property of objects—it is a wavelength of light, focused by the eye and interpreted by the brain. As we have seen, what Wordsworth means by the word 'Nature' is not something 'out there' separate from man, it is an *interaction* of external stimuli and the perceiving mind. We are, in a most literal and scientific sense, a *part* of Nature. It is our half-creation. The 'motion and a spirit' that 'rolls through all things' is interfused with both the world of natural beauty, and the 'mind of man' that recognizes that beauty. 'Tintern Abbey' takes the two worlds, inner and outer, at their point of intersection: for Wordsworth the 'language of the sense' is not just a matter of aesthetics, or optics, or philosophy, or psychology, but *poetry*—which involves them all: we perceive not merely scenes, we perceive *values*:

> Therefore am I still
> A lover of the meadows and the woods,
> And mountains; and of all that we behold
> From this green earth; of all the mighty world
> Of eye and ear, both what they half-create,
> And what perceive; well pleased to recognize
> In nature and the language of the sense,
> The anchor of my purest thoughts, the nurse,
> The guide, the guardian of my heart, and soul
> Of all my moral being.   (ll. 103–12)

But for Wordsworth the central problem of 'Tintern Abbey' is that these moments of visionary union with Nature, when the poet becomes specifically conscious of the unity of which he is always a part, are never lasting. They come and go, and we are left only with the memory to

[20] See M. Rader, *Wordsworth: A Philosophical Approach*, 41–8.

sustain us. Hence the importance of these 'spots of time', and the recollection of them in tranquillity when their memory seems to feed and nourish the mind.

There is a terrible irony in the last part of the poem as Wordsworth turns from the contemplation of his own past failure and recovery to pay loving tribute to his sister Dorothy. Without her, as he recognizes, he would probably never have been a poet. In particular, she was perhaps the vital catalyst in the creation of the *Lyrical Ballads*. Without her presence that gloomy November evening in 1797 the 'The Ancient Mariner', and perhaps the whole volume might never have existed—and certainly not in the form in which it did. Wordsworth's great tribute to her and prayer for her future which occupy that last 50 lines of the poem are fully deserved:

> Oh! yet a little while
> May I behold in thee what I was once,
> My dear, dear Sister! And this prayer I make,
> Knowing that Nature never did betray
> The heart that loved her; 'tis her privilege,
> Through all the years of this our life, to lead
> From joy to joy . . .
>   Oh! then,
> If solitude, or fear, or pain, or grief,
> Should be thy portion, with what healing thoughts
> Of tender joy wilt thou remember me,
> And these my exhortations! (ll. 120–6; 143–7)

Everyone who knew Dorothy as she was in 1798 mentions, not her looks—she was never a beauty—but her sparkling vitality, and above all the bright 'wild' eyes her brother picks out in line 152. In 1829 she, who had done so much to help William's recovery, had an even more serious breakdown herself. The last twenty-six years of her life until her death in 1855 were spent in the grip of a nervous or neurotic illness so severe as to make her partially or completely insane. Whether or not, as Wordsworth's biographer argues,[21] Nature was indeed a comfort to her in her affliction, for him the irony must have been hard to bear.

It is often dangerous to draw too heavily on biographical background to understand poetry, yet Wordsworth is so deliberately a poet of his own life that we can scarcely avoid it in 'Tintern Abbey'. For all the bitter irony of the ending there is a sense in which his own life did prove him right. If we see 'Tintern Abbey' not as a promise of security for the

[21] Moorman I, 407.

future (something we can never have) but as a poem about Wordsworth's recovery and growth, then I think we see it in its proper perspective. The love of Nature is not an insurance policy; it was for Wordsworth the making of a poet from a disappointed and broken idealist—but to be a poet is to live dangerously, and by brief and passing achievements. 'Tintern Abbey' is not about a lifetime, but a moment of vision on an anniversary. It brings past and future into a single focus: a moment of intense awareness that made an anniversary in one man's life of universal significance. In this sense it shows us what the entire *Lyrical Ballads* were striving to do. When the Romantic poets or critics described a work of art as possessing 'organic unity' they were borrowing an image from a living body. The parts, however complex they might be individually, were only to be understood finally in terms of the 'life' of the whole. The whole body is, therefore greater than the sum of its parts. 'We murder to dissect.' Conversely, each part changes the nature of the whole, and therefore of all the other parts. 'Tintern Abbey', for instance, shows us the vision of Nature that lies behind 'Expostulation and Reply'; it provides an answer and a reassurance to the metaphysical terror of 'The Ancient Mariner'. In one sense it was apparently an afterthought, yet with hindsight we can see how it helped on the one hand to reshape the entire structure of the *Lyrical Ballads* in 1798, and, on the other, how its stress on 'spots of time' points forward to Wordsworth's next and greatest poetic achievement, *The Prelude*.

3   What is a Poet?

Wordsworth's Preface to the 1800 edition of the *Lyrical Ballads*, with its additions of 1802, is an integral part of the whole scheme—that is, if we read it chronologically *backwards*. It is not so much that Wordsworth's ideas about poetry change and develop between 1798, when he wrote his original brief Advertisement for the first edition, and 1802, when he appended the lengthy section to his 1800 Preface on 'What is a Poet?', but that we see him at work over these four years searching for, and trying to put into words, his first principles. We are watching him, as it were, stripping back his ideas like the layers of an onion. Beneath each argument there lie further unstated assumptions on which it depends. These must, in their turn, be uncovered, articulated, and examined, as Wordsworth attempts to define with greater and greater clarity *why* what he and Coleridge had done initially so instinctively and unconsciously in putting together that collection of poems in 1798 had created such a radical result. In the original Advertisement he had been content to describe the poems as 'experiments'—'written chiefly with a view to ascertain how far the language of conversation in the middle and lower classes of society is adapted for the purposes of poetic pleasure'.[1] The aim was to give a 'natural delineation of human passions, human characters, and human incidents'. By 1800 this tentative suggestion that ordinary speech might be the best poetic vehicle for revealing the basic human passions is expanded into a theory of language and poetic diction, accompanied by a theoretical disquisition on the consequent difference between verse and prose. Even here, however, Wordsworth clearly fails to find a bedrock of unassailable first principles, and so in 1802 he goes on to uncover the foundation-stone beyond which no enquiry, he believes, is possible. The answer to his question, 'What is poetry?' is to be found not in the properties of language after all, but in the essential nature of the poet himself. His aesthetic position is best understood therefore if, as I have suggested, we work chronologically backwards, starting with this basic premise and referring the rest of the theoretical superstructure to its base.

[1] *Lyrical Ballads*, 7.

If we needed to try to show that the Preface does express the principles of the first edition, and is not an afterthought, or even a modification of the original conception, we would have to look no further than Wordsworth's idea of a poet. In anchoring the discussion of poetry in the character of the poet himself, Wordsworth is adopting a position that is characteristic of Romanticism in nearly all its forms.[2] What marks the aesthetic theory of Wordsworth and Coleridge off from so many other Romantics, however, is that the poet is seen in radically *egalitarian* terms.

> What is a Poet? . . . He is a man speaking to men: a man, it is true,
> endued with more lively sensibility, more enthusiasm and tenderness,
> who has a greater knowledge of human nature, and a more
> comprehensive soul, than are supposed to be common among
> mankind; a man pleased with his own passions and volitions, and who
> rejoices more than other men in the spirit of life that is in him;
> delighting to contemplate similar volitions and passions as manifested
> in the goings-on of the Universe, and habitually impelled to create
> them where he does not find them.[3]

Unlike so many later European Romantics, for whom Byron was to appear the archetypal poet-figure, Wordsworth does not see the poet as a man set aside from the rest of humanity by his talent and calling. 'He is a man speaking to men.' The artist is more fully 'human' than his contemporaries, in that what is potential or latent in them is actualized and fulfilled in him. He is a representative man, not an outcast. He *shares* his 'greater knowledge' and more 'comprehensive soul' with his fellows. 'Among the qualities which I have enumerated as principally conducing to form a Poet, is implied nothing differing in kind from other men, but only in degree.'[4] In his *Biographia Literaria* Coleridge, for much the same reasons as he and Wordsworth acted upon in writing the *Lyrical Ballads*, insisted that the 'Secondary Imagination' of the creative artist differs only 'in *degree* and in the *mode* of its operation' from the 'Primary Imagination', which is, in effect, the normal power of sense-perception in all human beings.[5] We are all of us potential artists—and the artist shows us what we might be. Critics have called attention to the fact that Coleridge's account of the Primary and Secondary Imaginations is borrowed from Schelling. None of them, to my knowledge, have pointed out that on *this*

---

[2] See M. H. Abrams, *The Mirror and the Lamp*, ch. I.
[3] *Lyrical Ballads*, 255.
[4] *Ibid.*, 261.
[5] *Biographia Literaria*, ed. J. Shawcross, I, 202.

issue he stands Schelling on his head. The German implies that the special powers of the artist enable him to perceive a *different* world from that of the ordinary person;[6] Coleridge declares his faith that the artist sees and shares in the same world as the rest of humanity. Like the Ancient Mariner, his experiences send him back 'To walk together to the Kirk / With a goodly company'. The egalitarianism of Wordsworth and Coleridge was not just political and aesthetic: behind it was a religious vision of the fatherhood of God, and the brotherhood of man.

Poetry, for Wordsworth, is therefore something that binds men together, bringing into play both intellect and passion; though it is rooted in the particular, it emphasizes what is common and general to mankind:

> Aristotle, I have been told, hath said, that Poetry is the most philosophic of all writing: it is so: its object is truth, not individual and local, but general and operative; not standing upon external testimony, but carried alive into the heart by passion. . . .[7]

His informant on the subject of Aristotle (presumably Coleridge?) was not quite correct, but, as Wordsworth's casual admission of hearsay shows, the point is immaterial. The important thing is that it is his own view. What *is* interesting is the meaning he attaches to this word 'philosophic'. He is using it in a sense close to its root: 'loving of wisdom'. It is the perception of 'truth' not merely in any intellectual sense, but embracing both fact and feeling. It is a startling usage for us today—as indeed is his whole emphasis on the *generality* of poetry. Wordsworth never lost his belief—more common to eighteenth-century thinkers than Romantics—that all men, everywhere, were really very much alike under the superficial divisions of race, class and culture. General truth was that immediately recognizable to all. It is easy to see how this 'uniformitarianism' goes with his egalitarian and democratic beliefs; it was not until the middle of the nineteenth century that an increasing weight of anthropological and historical evidence began to stress how wide were the gulfs that could separate one culture, or one historical period from another. Similarly, the 'philosophic' unity of poetry extended, Wordsworth believed, to all areas of human endeavour.

> 'Poetry is the first and last of all knowledge—it is as immortal as the heart of man. If the labours of men of Science should ever create any material revolution, direct or indirect, in our condition, and in the

[6] *Ibid.*, 272; G. N. G. Orsini, *Coleridge and German Idealism* (Southern Illinois University Press 1969), 225–8.

[7] *Lyrical Ballads*, 259.

impressions which we habitually receive, the Poet will sleep then no
more than at present, but he will be ready to follow the steps of the
Man of Science, not only in those general indirect effects, but he will
be at his side, carrying sensation into the midst of the objects of the
Science itself.[8]

Like 'philosophy', the word 'science' has a broader meaning for
Wordsworth's day than for our own. For the eighteenth century a 'Man
of Science' is one who possesses knowledge in any area of learning, or
skill in any craft, rather than merely in the natural sciences. But
Wordsworth's next sentence makes it plain that he *is* referring primarily
to the physical sciences. His distinction is between knowledge that is
merely known by the head, and that which is felt by the whole person:
that which is 'palpably material to us as enjoying and suffering beings'. As
T. S. Eliot has remarked in an exactly parallel context, the poet feels his
thought 'as immediately as the odour of a rose'.

> When a poet's mind is perfectly equipped for its work, it is
> constantly amalgamating disparate experience; the ordinary man's
> experience is chaotic, irregular, fragmentary. The latter falls in love,
> or reads Spinoza, and these two experiences have nothing to do with
> each other, or with the noise of a typewriter or the smell of cooking;
> in the mind of the poet these experiences are always forming new
> wholes.[9]

It is this vision of the *unity* of the poet's sensibility that underlies
Wordsworth's conception of 'poetry'. From it stem the two main themes
of his 1800 Preface: firstly, that poetry is 'the spontaneous overflow of
powerful feelings'; and, secondly, that the language of poetry is the
language of ordinary men.

By using the phrase 'spontaneous overflow' Wordsworth is implicitly
comparing poetry to a fountain—welling up of its own accord from deep
emotion. This is not to imply that it is like 'automatic writing', or that
care, craftsmanship, and patient revision are not essential. Few poets have
laboured harder or more consciously at their craft than Wordsworth, and
none have subjected their work to more frequent revision—sometimes,
as in the case of *The Prelude*, or 'The Female Vagrant', over a period of
many years. We do not always realize how paradoxical is a belief in
poetry as 'the spontaneous overflow of powerful feelings' that 'takes its
origin from emotion recollected in tranquillity'. The paradox is

[8] *Lyrical Ballads*, 259–60.
[9] 'The Metaphysical Poets', *Selected Essays*, 3rd edn (London 1951), 287.

deliberate—and one that is central to understanding Romantic poetry. Wordsworth is describing his own experience of writing poetry: its creation is both spontaneous and free, yet simultaneously fiercely controlled and disciplined by the conscious judgement of the poet. It is not a question of 'either/or' but 'both': each demands its opposite. Poetry is like a magnet: it cannot exist without *both* poles. Wordsworth's vision of the unified sensibility of the poet is essentially dialectical. He was, as he tells us in the *Prelude*, 'foster'd alike by beauty and by fear'. As we have already seen, the poetry of the *Lyrical Ballads* exists under tension—but as Wordsworth is careful to insist, its product is 'pleasure' and 'delight'. Even when, as here, he is at his most radical, he still writes within a conscious tradition of aesthetics that reaches back through Johnson and Dryden to Sidney, and beyond. Like his forebears, Wordsworth sees the purpose of poetry to 'instruct through pleasing'. As are all great innovators, Wordsworth was free of the provincialism of the contemporary. He cannot write without being aware of the whole tradition of English poetry of which he has become a part. 'If my conclusions are admitted,' he writes, 'and carried as far as they must be carried if admitted at all, our judgements concerning the works of the greatest Poets both ancient and modern will be far different from what they are at present.'[10] Wordsworth does not intend any iconoclasm here. The purpose of his radically new aesthetic of dialectic and tension is essentially *conservative*. He wishes to restore and revitalize what he sees as the great tradition of English poetry:

> The invaluable works of our elder writers, I had almost said the works of Shakespeare and Milton, are driven into neglect by frantic novels, sickly and stupid German Tragedies, and deluges of idle and extravagant stories in verse.—When I think upon this degrading thirst after outrageous stimulation I am almost ashamed to have spoken of the feeble effort with which I have endeavoured to counteract it; and reflecting upon the magnitude of the general evil, I should be oppressed with no dishonorable melancholy, had I not a deep impression of certain inherent and indestructible qualities of the human mind . . .[11]

As we have said, the theory of poetic diction is similarly rooted in Wordsworth's idea of a poet as a 'man speaking to men' who reveals to his fellows the hidden unity of their experience. 'The poet thinks and feels in the spirit of the passions of men. How, then, can his language differ in

[10] *Lyrical Ballads*, 255.
[11] *Ibid.*, 249.

any material degree from that of all other men who feel vividly and see clearly?'[12] Wordsworth's views on the greater sincerity and emotional depth of the rural poor have already been mentioned, but it is a cornerstone of his theory:

> Low rustic life was generally chosen because in that situation the essential passions of the heart find a better soil in which they can attain their maturity, are less under restraint, and speak a plainer and more emphatic language; because in that situation our elementary feelings exist in a state of greater simplicity and consequently may be more accurately contemplated and more forcibly communicated. . . . The language too of these men is adopted . . . because such men hourly communicate with the best objects from which the best part of language is originally derived. . . .[13]

Wordsworth is here at his most primitivistic. He saw in the rustic, as it were, the basic human type from which all others are derived. The task of the poet is to reunite the sophisticated reader with his roots, and to bring him back to purer more simple ways of feeling and expressing himself. It is a mark of our social deracination, Wordsworth believed, that we have come to despise our primitive selves. The oppression of the poor by the rich reflects the alienation of the rich from their own deepest feelings.

Stated thus, Wordsworth's theory of poetic diction is attractive and even plausible, but some of its implications were less so—and it is this notion more than any other part of the Preface that drew Coleridge's critical fire in later years. In Chapter XVII of *Biographia Literaria* he points out the contradiction between Wordsworth's belief in the inherent superiority of the rural poor and his uniformitarianism: What is valuable in Wordsworth's poetic rustics is not their rusticity but their universality—but if their important qualities are common to all men, they cannot also be peculiar to one class. Similarly, to the question of the quality of language used by such people, Coleridge continues, quoting the passage cited above,

> . . . I reply; that a rustic's language, purified from all provincialism and grossness, and so far reconstructed as to be made consistent with the rules of grammar (which are in essence no other than the laws of universal logic, applied to psychological materials) will not differ from the language of any other man of common-sense, however

[12] *Ibid.*, 261.
[13] *Ibid.*, 245.

learned or refined he may be, except as far as the notions, which the rustic has to convey, are fewer and more indiscriminate.[14]

But Coleridge goes on, there *is* a very real distinction between the language of the educated and the uneducated that Wordsworth has chosen to ignore completely. This is that the uneducated all too often lack the vital qualities of discrimination, selection, and generalization necessary for clear communication. Ask a peasant to describe an event and you are told *everything*. All information enjoys an equal status; facts are not organized according to any principles of relevance. There is no overall plan.[15] Fortunately, as Coleridge points out with some satisfaction, Wordsworth does not often allow the linguistic egalitarianism of his theories to interfere with 'the processes of genuine imagination' in his poetry. Even 'The Thorn' and 'The Last of the Flock', though they may use the words of common speech, do not follow normal word orders or syntax.

All this, however, is by way of introduction to his attack on Wordsworth's major theoretical proposition, that 'There neither is or can be any essential difference between the language of prose and metrical composition.' 'Now prose itself,' declares Coleridge, '. . . differs, and ought to differ, from the language of conversation; even as reading ought to differ from talking.'[16]

> The true question must be, whether there are not modes of expression, a *construction*, and an *order* of sentences, which are in their fit and natural place in a serious prose composition, but would be disproportionate and heterogeneous in metrical poetry; and vice versa, whether in the language of a serious poem there may not be an arrangement both of words and sentences, and a use and selection of (what are called) *figures of speech*, both as to their kind, their frequency, and their occasions, which on a subject of equal weight would be vicious and alien in correct and manly prose. I contend that in both cases this unfitness of each for the place of the other will and ought to exist.[17]

Concluding a lengthy series of examples of metrical structure, Coleridge throws down his own counter-contention 'that there is, and ought to be

[14] *Biographia Literaria*, II, 38.
[15] *Ibid.*, 44.
[16] *Ibid.*, 45.
[17] *Ibid.*, 49.

an *essential* difference between the language of prose and of metrical composition'.[18]

Coleridge's attack on Wordsworth's theory of poetic diction is relentless in its highlighting of each new absurdity and complication into which Wordsworth's all-embracing theory seems to precipitate him. Yet he desires neither to mock nor to score off his old friend and co-author. Coleridge is, in fact, faced with a problem of some difficulty, and in tackling it we see his greatness as a critic. He had seen, perhaps more clearly than any of his contemporaries, Wordsworth's true genius as a poet and critical theorist, but he is increasingly baffled by the apparently wilful wrong-headedness of certain parts of Wordsworth's poetic theory. The uniqueness of Coleridge's literary biography is that it is not primarily about himself at all, but about his attempts to understand Wordsworth. The driving force behind the whole of *Biographia Literaria* is Coleridge's need to reject Wordsworth's aesthetics, and to construct a new system that will do adequate justice to both his critical theory and his poetic genius. The discussion of Wordsworth's Preface is thus not a Coleridgean digression (of which, in a narrow sense, *Biographia Literaria* has many) but a central stage in his argument. His disagreement with Wordsworth over the nature of metre and diction must be seen against the background of common principles and poetic ideals which they had shared in 1798—and still shared in 1817 when he wrote the *Biographia*. The *Biographia* is, in effect, a continuation of the creative tension that had always been present in the poets' relationship, and which had come to its first flowering that November evening in 1797. Coleridge is criticizing Wordsworth's theories in part in order that he may show the genius of the whole:

> Yet so groundless does this system appear on a close examination; and so strange and overwhelming its consequences, that I cannot, and do not, believe that the poet did ever himself adopt it in the unqualified sense, in which his expressions have been understood by others, and which, indeed, according to all the common laws of interpretation they seem to bear.[19]

Wordsworth, he reminds us, was in reaction against the inane or gaudy affectations of popular poetry of the day. His real objective was a verse that *by its artifice* gave an impression of 'naturalness' and colloquial ease, while retaining the dignity, the compression, the depth of feeling, and the clarity of ideas that we associate with the highest poetry. This 'simplicity'

[18] *Ibid.*, 57.
[19] *Ibid.*, 69.

of Wordsworth is not a product of genuine adherence to the speech-patterns of yokels, but of the most sophisticated poetic technique—just as Shakespeare's blank verse gives an illusion of ordinary speech when we are caught up in the world of the play. Moreover, Coleridge adds, this ability of Wordsworth's is essentially a *traditional* quality of English poetry. It is a skill common alike to Chaucer and to George Herbert. But, impressive as this ability of Wordsworth's is, it is not the 'characteristic excellence' of his style, says Coleridge with a charming back-handed compliment, since he has other and 'higher powers.'[20]

> To me it will always remain a singular and noticeable fact; that a theory which would establish this *lingua communis*, not only as the best, but as the only commendable style, should have proceeded from a poet, whose diction, next to that of Shakespeare and Milton, appear to me of all others the most *individualized* and characteristic.[21]

For all its assumption of the language of ordinary men, Wordsworth's poetry is as unmistakably individual in its own way as that of other great poets. Whatever he writes, whether in his own person, or in the guise of some other character, it is always Wordsworth's voice that is heard. If this results sometimes in a weakness of characterization, that is because, for all his theories, 'the natural *tendency* of the poet's mind is to great objects and elevated conceptions.'[22] In attempting to give significance to the small and trivial, says Coleridge, Wordsworth is like a swan out of water which 'having amused himself, for a while, with crushing the weeds on the river's bank, soon returns to his own majestic movements on its reflecting and sustaining surface'.[23] The contrast between the flat-footed waddling of the swan over the weeds and its grandeur on the water sums up the gap between the work written in response to theory and Wordsworth's greatest poetry better than many critical essays.

But for all their brilliance and insight, we must beware of accepting Coleridge's criticisms of Wordsworth uncritically. He is riding a hobby-horse as much as Wordsworth. He believes that Wordsworth's true vocation is not the production of short lyrics, cramped by absurd theories, but the Great Philosophic Poem of which he alone was capable—in short, the unfinished and never-to-be-finished *Recluse*. In pursuit of this fantasy of his own Coleridge is—as we have seen—less than fair to the quality of the best of the *Lyrical Ballads*. The 'Anecdote for

[20] *Ibid.*, 77.
[21] *Ibid.*, 77.
[22] *Ibid.*, 96.
[23] *Ibid.*, 96–7.

Fathers', 'Expostulation and Reply', and 'The Tables Turned', do use simple ordinary language without sacrificing intellectual or emotional subtlety—even if their syntax is not quite that of ordinary rustic conversation.

Finally, we turn back to the outermost layer of the onion—the original Advertisement to the 1798 *Ballads*. Having worked backwards from 1802 we are now better able to see in what sense the *Lyrical Ballads* are 'experiments'. It is not just that the individual poems themselves are committed to living dangerously—to show the sublime in the commonplace even while insisting on its commonplaceness. Wordsworth and Coleridge are experimenting in the relationship of reader and author. 'It is supposed', wrote Wordsworth in 1800, 'that by the act of writing in verse an Author makes a formal engagement that he will gratify certain known habits of association.'[24] The *Lyrical Ballads* are the opening shot in an all-out campaign against that supposition. In their extreme simplicity they are *meant* to be difficult. In the *Biographia* Coleridge reserves his choicest scorn for those who find Wordsworth's poetry easy. But, as the Preface makes abundantly clear, the *Ballads* are not merely a conscious innovation. They are aimed at something much more innovative: the creation of a consciousness of the nature and meaning of artistic innovation. The authors for all their clumsy anonymity, are declaring themselves in a new kind of way, and attempting to show the world in a new kind of light. Poetry is not a matter of verbal felicity and decoration. It has a message—as Keats was to complain, 'a palpable design upon us'. Poetry, for Wordsworth and Coleridge, was about transforming men's consciousness. 'Tintern Abbey', like 'The Ancient Mariner', is about a radical change of heart.

[24] *Lyrical Ballads*, 243.

Bibliography

All references to the *Lyrical Ballads* or to Wordsworth's Preface are given to the edition edited by R. L. Brett and A. E. Jones (London 1963, revised 1965).

The number of critical works about Wordsworth and Coleridge is legion. For convenience I am listing below a few that seem to me to be of help to the ordinary student, and refer substantially to the poems or background of the *Lyrical Ballads* in particular rather than to Wordsworth and Coleridge in general. Most, but not all, will have been mentioned in my text. Some books mentioned in the text do not appear below since they are only of interest in the limited context where they are cited (e.g. Charles Wesley's *Hymns*). Also for convenience, if contemporary documents are easily available through secondary sources I have not bothered to give the primary (e.g. reviews of the *Lyrical Ballads* are referred to appendix C of Brett's edition).

Abrams, M. H., *The Mirror and the Lamp* (New York 1953).

Coleridge, Samuel Taylor, *Biographia Literaria*, ed. J. Shawcross (London 1907).

—— *The Friend*, ed. B. E. Rooke (London 1969).

—— *Table Talk*, ed. H. N. Coleridge (London 1852).

—— *The Critical Heritage*, ed. R. R. de J. Jackson (London 1972).

Hanson, Lawrence, *Life of S. T. Coleridge* (London 1938).

Fruman, Norman, *Coleridge, the Damaged Archangel* (London 1972).

Harding, D. W., 'The Theme of "The Ancient Mariner"', *Scrutiny*, IX, 1941.

House, Humphry, *Coleridge* (London 1953).

Legouis, Emile, *The Early Life of Wordsworth*, trans. —— Matthews (London 1897).

Lowes, J. Livingstone, *The Road to Xanadu* (Boston 1927).

Moorman, Mary, *William Wordsworth: The Early Years* (London 1957).

—— *William Wordsworth: The Later Years* (London 1965).

Prickett, Stephen, *Coleridge and Wordsworth: The Poetry of Growth* (London 1970).

Rader, Melvin, *Wordsworth, A Philosophical Approach* (London 1967).

Warren, Robert Penn, 'A Poem of Pure Imagination', *Selected Essays* (London 1964).

Wordsworth, Dorothy, *Journals*, ed. E. de Selincourt (London 1941).

Wordsworth, William, *Letters of William and Dorothy Wordsworth, The Early Years, 1787–1805*, 2nd edn. eds. E. de Selincourt and C. L. Shaver (London 1967).

—— *Poetical Works*, ed. E. de Selincourt, 5 vols. (London 1940–49).

STIRLING
DISTRICT
LIBRARY

Index